The Substitute Teacher Effect

The Substitute Teacher Effect

A novel study on student misbehavior in school

SAMMY KAYES

The Substitute Teacher Effect,
Second edition

Artwork in the final pages by Ricardo Hernandez.
Images and captions used with permission of the artist.

ISBN:0692676805
ISBN-13:9780692676806

File under: Education / Theory and Social Aspects

Special thanks to TSJ book club for reading and feedback.

The Substitute Teacher Effect

Table of Contents

Preface

Ahh, substitute teaching. Who *wouldn't* want to do it? (There are dozens of us.) After completing my student teaching in the fall of 2013, I decided to become a substitute teacher in the Chicago Public Schools district. This would be a temporary prospect; I certainly didn't go through a several-year-long teacher certification program to be a lifetime "sub." Substitute teaching, though, would give me the time that I felt I still needed. I did not expect that I would quickly find the position I wanted, nor did I have full confidence in my ideas. Subbing would give me precious extra time, but not only that, it would give me insight, practice, and experience while paying the bills.

Within several months, I had already found a greater purpose in this side quest. Though one goal of subbing was to become a better teacher, it happened that gradually I would become more obsessed with the phenomenon that I called *the substitute teacher effect*. Going to all these different schools, trying out new techniques, interviewing teachers, students, and staff—this would be a way to improve myself—but even more, I'd learn about the student psyche.

The psyche, though, does not exist in isolation of schools and our society. It is directly related to its surrounding conditions. In other words, students' attitudes are affected by our schooling practices, and the environment of schools—as well as our broader social environment and cultural values. Eventually, I would come to believe that the psychology of "the substitute teacher effect" revealed a systemic set of beliefs about learning, living, and even the social order.

I must acknowledge that my experience as a substitute teacher has been predominantly in high schools, with most students below the poverty line. Poverty also tends to be more correlated with black and Latino students than Asians and whites. Although I have also observed, studied, and been a student in non-poor and non-segregated schools, I will concede that my observations, and my theory, are probably more true (more often) in this general context of poor and minority students in the United States of America in the early 21st century.

With that said, the issues discussed in this book are, to some degree, evident from early childhood education to the graduate-level; rich to poor; black to white. I believe that in this book I've examined a phenomenon which is rooted in our own history and culture—and a general conception of school, learning, and children.

Finally, I would propose to my readers, especially those who are educators, that they critique and improve upon my work and this general theory of "the substitute teacher effect." I wrote this book because no book on the topic could be found. I wrote it—not because I have all the answers, but because I want us to have the discussion in the first place.

What I can certainly promise is that the experiences recounted in this book are accurate, and my beliefs honest.

Introduction

What is the substitute teacher effect? I believe everyone knows. Ask anyone the question: "What happens when students have a substitute teacher?" and their answers will be similar. Although the "substitute teacher effect" depends somewhat on the school, and a variety of other factors—the differences will be more "quantitative" than "qualitative." In other words, the substitute teacher effect is a fundamental element of life in our school system—much like desks, lockers, and extracurricular activities. It's just what students do, and it exists on a scale of "more or less" rather than "happens or doesn't happen."

A good illustration of the substitute teacher effect can be found in the book *Substitute Teacher from the Black Lagoon*, by Mike Thaler. On the first page, students realize the teacher is sick, and that they're going to "have a sub." The next several pages show the classroom a mess, with the students running around, jumping on desks, doing handstands, and kicking the teacher's apple off the desk. The students even re-write the emergency lesson plan: instead of "learning," they will order a pizza and tie the substitute teacher to a wooden plank.

"This is party time!" they proclaim.

"Call 911!" yells the substitute teacher.

Though an exaggeration of most cases—(and possibly an understatement of certain cases)—this is the substitute teacher effect.

What ends up straightening out the students is a scary monster sub from the black lagoon. And though

Mike Thaler's book has a happier ending than I expected, in the real world it rarely ends on this kind of happy note. As evident in classroom management methods, "control through fear" is the prevailing solution to student chaos.

But what *causes* the substitute teacher effect? Now that is a question rarely asked. It is rarely asked because the answer is assumed to be known and obvious (childhood, of course), or that it doesn't even matter.

I do not believe the question has been fully answered, and I believe the answer does matter. It matters not simply because it annoys us substitute teachers, but because this "problem" is merely the tip of an iceberg. The substitute teacher effect is a problem of its own, but it would be more meaningful to say it is a symptom of many larger problems. It is a visible sign of every thing, small and large, that contributes to "bad" student attitudes about school and their world in general. The substitute teacher's perspective is a rare window into what is wrong, and it potentially leads into a deeper understanding of the real problems.

Beneath the surface of this iceberg, we find apathy, irrelevance, and poor general health. *The substitute teacher effect*, I believe, is a manifestation of these other, deeper problems.

These problems are not quite the fault of the students, are they? It would be difficult to blame students for their "bad" behaviors if we first realized that most their behaviors are learned from adults; and also that "bad behavior" is a common response to hunger, boredom, loneliness, fear, anger, upset, sickness, or even just a sense of unfairness. And so in this book, I ultimately ask: what is causing the students to rebel? Because that's what they are doing—and they are doing it on a systematic basis. I would say it surely has something to do with these kind of feelings.

It's more complex than simply "bad attitudes." When we're talking about the substitute teacher effect, there must be something more at play. Parents and regular teachers experience "bad" behavior, too. Why is it that students are notoriously "worse" when it is the *substitute* teacher? What is it about the *substitute* teacher that makes the students fly off the handle?

The first question I would ask is whether "behaviors" are a reliable indicator of much at all. I would suggest that they are somewhat reliable—in some situations—in order to make certain predictions, estimations, and generalizations. But they are ultimately unreliable for understanding what a student is actually thinking or feeling. Of course that's true, right? Even if we do not always act on this implicit knowledge, or form our policies and practices based around it—behaviors do not actually tell us what is on someone's mind or in someone's heart. They can only *suggest* what a person is thinking or feeling—and sometimes, these suggestions are misleading. A simple illustration would be the student who is sitting quietly at his or her desk, "doing their work," quite peacefully—and the moment the regular teacher leaves the room, this same student will get up and loudly run around the classroom. The substitute teacher, you see, has a look behind the scenes.

Because of the substitute teacher's unique position, he/she can gain insight. The *difference* in a student's behavior—in the presence of the regular teacher vs. the substitute teacher—is a message of its own. Why do students "typically" act one way, and then, when a different person is "in charge," act another way?

Part of the answer lies in the students' response to authority, including how students operate when there is *less* authority. When we examine the substitute teacher effect, it becomes more clear why students act differently for the substitute teacher: the sub is not perceived nearly as much as an authority. Ok, so this makes perfect sense, and is something everyone knows. *But why do students need "authority" to "behave" or "do the assignment?"* I'd propose three big reasons:

#1 Students do not have the mental, emotional, physical, and/or psychological capacity.

#2 Students do not have a good ethical sense, or the right kind of values.

#3 "What" students are being "asked to do" is not personally relevant, interesting, ethical, and/or developmentally appropriate.

I would argue that these reasons occur regularly in combination. As for the first two, these certainly have a correlation with "childhood," yet at the same time say something about what we *do not* teach them—at home, in school, and culturally. It is not a fact of "nature" that students, even young students, must be bad at making ethical/intelligent decisions—and conducting themselves without an adult, on their own. At least as often, it would be a matter of "failing to nurture." All three of these elements are affected by our school and social priorities. Reason three seems almost taboo to bring up.

There is a huge problem when students act differently under authority and when *free* of authority. Ultimately, it comes down to the reasons we teach them—whether implicitly or explicitly—to act or not to act. One major issue here is that students are consistently trained to obey, rather than develop sophisticated judgment. And so, they develop a need for someone to enforce the law—including when, how, and why to "learn." Obedience is consistently our solution, but it tends to create more problems than it solves, because it removes people from the responsibility to think for themselves.

Our institutions, despite the well-intentioned teachers and caring parents who work with them, train students in multiple ways to only act or not act when they are told or not told. The students do not consistently develop reasons of their own to be calm, to have respect, or to learn. And if they do, it is usually in spite of the system—not because of it.

Their behavior certainly isn't all conscious. As previously mentioned, there are factors out of the students' control that affect them. Who do you think is more likely to act out: a hungry student, or a student who isn't hungry? Who is more likely to have trouble staying in their seat: a dancer, or someone who likes to read books all day? Who is more likely to *want* to work on their assignment: a student who has been given a choice in what they are doing, or a student who has absolutely no say in the matter? The deck is stacked against all children, but some of them more than others. And this illustrates how "bad" behaviors are often not morally "bad," but simply inconvenient to authority. If the rules were bad in the first place, the behaviors are not necessarily bad if they break the bad rule.

I ask you: if you loved what you were doing; thought you were being treated fairly; knew how to think and act for yourself; and had your needs taken care of—why would you ever rebel? Even if you had a different adult in the room? We could probably agree that it would be less frequent and less systematic. In my experience, there is a clear correlation between the severity of "the substitute teacher effect" and factors such as "how we treat them" and "if we are providing for them."

We're doing lots of stuff wrong, and the "substitute teacher effect," I believe, is just one tell. The students' "behaviors" are far less of a concern for me than *why* the students are behaving this way in the first place.

Part I

Enter, Substitute Teacher

1. It's time to get away

> "I want to get away.
>
> I want to fly away....
>
> (yeah, yeah, yeah,)
>
> I want to *get away!*"

Remember the popular 90's anthem by Lenny Kravitz? The substitute teacher knows what this song is about. It is about the students who will fly high in the sky, metaphorically speaking, when they realize their teacher is gone for the day.

Not really, but it might as well be. I spent years observing students from a novel point of view, working with them, and occasionally, asking them questions about this very phenomenon of the substitute teacher effect. Let's go through a typical day in my recent life as a substitute teacher, with side commentary.

1. I am in the classroom before the students arrive. This allows me to prepare myself, to prepare their assignment, and have it written on the board as they enter.

2. The bell rings, and the students will make their way to my class. I stand at the door as the students arrive. Sometimes, I will hold my clipboard at the door, with the attendance roster attached, and ask for their names/ID as they enter. Or sometimes I will simply greet them at the door, and then take attendance later. Either way, the students know that their regular teacher is gone, and I am the substitute teacher. At schools where I am unknown, the students will sometimes give a momentary look of confusion. But they catch on quickly. Some of them alert their friends to the big news.

As soon as they catch on, a good amount of them will smile, laugh, and/or dance. Many students appear way too happy that their teacher is gone, and that I am in their place. Some seem apathetic. Very few seem to be upset that class as they know it has been cancelled. A surprising amount of students have had "religious" experiences, as illustrated by the following actual quotes from students:

> *-Thank you Jesus! I didn't believe in God, but now I do.*
>
> *-My prayers have been answered.*
>
> *-You are my savior.*

I do not convert all of them by simply showing up. Some students will only tell me that I made their day, or that they are "soooo happy."

Many skeptics are already feeling skeptical of this book. That's fine. "Of course, there is a simple explanation for all this. You didn't need to write a book. **Kids just don't wanna learn stuff.**"

This is a critically mistaken assumption that I will be challenging through my work. It is simply false that people don't want to learn; what people *don't want* is to learn by force, without a choice, and/or when they are preoccupied with more urgent human thoughts and feelings.

Or another common one: "it's *the hormones.* Teenagers are rebellious by design." Many assumptions are built into this rationalization, the main one being that students are naturally like this—and it only follows that they will resist anything and everything. I believe this is another cultural myth that assumes too much about the nature of teenagers and people, overlooking "nurture" in the process.

Back to my day:

3. Most of the students will eventually sit in their seats. Rarely will they stop talking. Most will quickly have their phones out—and if "the sub" never says anything, the vast majority would talk to each other and be on their phones the entire period, despite most school/classroom rules.

Sometimes in the beginning of class, I would go around to each of the students, asking their names for attendance, and perhaps making small talk. I did this as a part of my attendance procedure because it was a little more personal, and also because I do not have a loud voice or overbearing demeanor. It takes a loud and proud stranger to call thirty teenagers to attention, and then hold them quiet for several minutes while you check off their names. Even for the loudest and proudest subs, this could be difficult. Just don't expect them all to stay quiet, the entire time, for a stranger on sub day—or you'll be disappointed. (Try it.)

4. During the course of my substitute teaching experience, I experimented with various ways of getting the students' attention, and then, directing them to their assignment. As I previously stated, it was a part of my procedure to have the assignment written on the board in the beginning of class. In schools where I was less known, I would make an effort to point this out to the students. In schools where I was more known, students knew (or should have known) that the assignment was always on the board.

Mostly, they did not care. Students rarely started anything on their own, and though it depends on circumstances, the truth is that it almost didn't matter which school or classroom I was in—the students would rarely do their assignment at all. The norm was to have 1-5 students in a class turn in their assignment at the end of the period, even if they knew it was due at the end, even if they knew it would be graded, even if I kept bothering them.

Although it was highly out of character, I would occasionally try being strict, and once or twice, I even tried yelling or being mean. I vowed to never do that again—but it was no more effective than being nice and patient. If anything, it was less effective. And if it was more effective, it would not be more effective at getting them to love learning and actually learn something from their assignment—it would only be more effective at getting them to pretend. "Doing work" does not mean "learning," and "learning" does not automatically translate into "meaningful learning."

(More on that later.)

And at the same time, students were conditioned to respond to yelling and harsh words. Students told me on several occasions that I needed to be meaner, I need to yell, I need to threaten them with "punishment." Lots of people would say that these are the strategies that "work," even though they are clearly inconsistent in how well they do "work." Even if strictness and rudeness do work sometimes, we must go further than asking what "works," and consider: "work to do *what?*" Training people to respond to negative consequences, first and foremost, ultimately endorses fear, anger, and authority itself—rather than judgment, respect, or love of learning. If we simply did whatever "worked," visibly and in the short-term, we'd end up with problems like students hating school, people hating authority, kids hating themselves, and a violent culture that must fight, threaten, punish, trick, and bribe to get what it wants.

Why do students want to do everything but their assignments?

I asked them often. And I got very good at making it clear that I will not punish them for their opinions, so I quickly gained students' trust, and they were typically honest with me in return. Their responses were consistent across a variety of schools and classrooms. Here are some of their responses:

-We don't have enough time to talk.

-The assignment is pointless and boring.

-I hate this.

-I'm too tired.

-When will we ever need to know this?

-What will I actually learn from this?

-We should be able to do what is interesting to us.

-I'll do it later.

-The teacher doesn't care.

-It's not graded.

-I already have a good grade.

-But it's just the substitute teacher.

Few would question the authenticity of these responses. I had absolutely no need to make any of them up, because they are so ordinary: we remember many of them ourselves, from our own childhood school experiences—and if we are a parent and/or teacher, we hear kids say these things all the time. It's nothing new to hear them. What would be actually different, though, is if we were to take the complaints seriously on a systemic level, and if we then saw these "complaints" as *feedback,* which we could use to improve ourselves, our culture, our school system.

In my teachers-for-social-justice book club meetings, I was once telling about some of my experiences as a substitute teacher, and I mentioned that the vast majority of the time, the assignments left behind for the students were worksheets. I saw this as some degree of a reflection of what teachers were doing in their own classes. Several practicing teachers commented that teachers sometimes do this because they do not know who the substitute teacher will be, and they do not have faith that the sub will be able to actually teach a lesson or oversee an assignment with more depth. One teacher used her own experience as an example. I thought this was a fair point. After this conversation, I would make a more consistent effort to ask students what their teachers normally did during class time. Many of them responded that it was the same thing during class time: worksheets were the norm in some classes, a part of daily operations. I also heard often that the teachers "talk too much."

In addition to my asking the students, I would occasionally have opportunities to sub for one of two teachers that shared a classroom. I could watch teachers as if it were a normal classroom day, and see how they normally taught. What did I see a lot of the time? For starters, I saw what the students told me: too much talking on the part of teachers, and too much sitting and listening on the part of students. Students were frequently reduced to passivity, silence, and following instructions. Many teachers, unfortunately, were very strict and rude to students—not necessarily because they're bad teachers/people, but because that's "how it works." And I saw too many worksheets.

What's the problem with worksheets, anyways?

The problem with worksheets is that they are pedantic and dissociated from virtually all real-world activities. Not only are they a bad tool for pedagogy, including the way in which they reduce students to quiet, passive obedience—they are even worse when we consider the effect of our practices on students' *desire* to learn and continue learning.

There we have it. One reason for the substitute teacher effect: leaving behind the worst kind of assignments from our toolbox. If worksheets are a mainstay in our regular classroom, that's even worse: the students will do everything they can to get away from them.

I can confirm that in classrooms where the teacher left behind instructions for the students to continue their personal projects, for example—there were less behavioral problems, and more students who were engaged and potentially learning.

But the rabbit hole goes way deeper than this. The dreaded worksheet, the lecture, the yelling and rudeness (which was only sometimes), are just a few examples of the things we do to turn students away from wanting to learn or "behave." The substitute teacher effect exists largely because we have given students a bad view of "learning"—in some way, and through various methods—and usually unintended. Our students have learned through the school, at home, and culturally, that "learning" is both painful and impersonal.

School is pain, work is pain, life is pain. Of course, they will want to get away from pain.

People also like doing things that relate to themselves

Not only is it more enjoyable to do things that you are interested in, you learn better that way. This really makes make sense if you get to thinking about it, and if you read what people like John Dewey had to say about learning and experience. But also this has become abundantly clear through scientific study of cognition in the mid-to-late 20th century. If you don't like something, or it doesn't relate to you, it's much less likely you're going to "learn" that thing. And if you do, it's not going to stay with you for very long. This is damning of worksheets, and curriculum that the students had no part in deciding. Even if students do their assignments, if they are not actually interested in it, they will be doing it because they have essentially been threatened with consequences. They will be going through the motions. This is not respectful to the learners' time, and they're not going to be learning much, anyways. The students' lack of desire to do their assignments—and their desire to do everything else instead—is a cue that we are approaching school in the entirely wrong way. If we can change our practices so that students' interests are more involved—rather than having to whip them into shape in order to get them to buckle down—we would undoubtedly see better results in attitudes and quality of learning.

The students want to get away because they think that they can. It is an opportunity to be subjected to less pain, and more freedom, which they typically are not granted. We must create schools and classrooms where the students do not want to get away in the first place; where "the sub" will be another person who can guide them, rather than someone whose enforcement of instructions they must subvert.

That was a long rant, but it felt necessary. These were some of the thoughts that were going through my mind as I was working on the job, and as I reflected later on my subbing experiences. Time for class to end:

5. The bell rings, and it is time for the students to leave. I might verbally wish them a nice rest of the day, and a few of them might respond back with enthusiasm. Some of the students are appreciative that I was kind and treated them with respect. I typically asked, rather than commanded. I acknowledged that they are free humans, not servants. Perhaps some of the students were even inspired. They are not going to let me teach the whole class, even if I have demonstrated that I could; but I can certainly work with them individually, and in small groups. If not on their assignment, then maybe something else intellectual, fun, and interesting.

"You are the best sub."

"We'll miss you."

"You should work here."

No, they don't all like me, and that's not even my goal. But I do know that if you are trusted and respected, people are more willing to listen and learn. If I return to this school as a sub, and if I have this class again, they still won't let me be their teacher—because that would interrupt their free time. It is an unwritten law in their subconscious student constitution which says that *sub day* equals *party time*, and nothing but hell freezing over will take that away from them. But it is not necessary to play sage on the stage, glue them to their seats, or make sure with the force of a tyrant that they fill-in-the-blank. I can still inspire them, and give them hope. Maybe I can even get them to consider that learning isn't all pain. And we'll go from there.

2. Sub's Dilemma

It might be difficult for some people to be a substitute teacher in a system where students are so strongly opposed to sitting still, being quiet, "doing work," and even "learning." Substitute teachers, even more than regular teachers, would quickly and easily come to believe that they must turn to harsher, stricter, crueller methods of adult-ing in order to get and keep the students "on task." The "regular" classroom teacher can at least develop a relationship with the students. The regular teacher has at least some power over curriculum and instruction—I say "some" because, if you weren't aware, teachers these days are under increasing political pressure and administrative restrictions with regard to what and how they teach.

The substitute teacher, on the other hand, is facing down the substitute teacher effect. The sub may have never seen the students before. The sub does not know typical procedures. The sub is not the one who created or assigned the assignment. And so, if the goal were simply to get the students to be productive, the substitute teacher would have to rely more on "authority" than things like "respect" and "mentoring." The two options for a sub might seem to be: "tyrannical" or "just give up."

Though I would occasionally give up—being a human with limited energy, optimism, and influence—I experimented with a third option. This third option was simply to attempt what the regular teacher would, despite unfamiliarity. It was an attempt at respect, inspiration, and mentoring. In the prevailing view, it seems that my job was simply to take attendance, get the students to "do their work" to some extent, and prevent catastrophe. But I wanted to use the time wisely when I could. One of the best strategies I would ever adopt was to ally myself with the students, rather than stand against them. In short, I refused to be a tyrant.

In generic wisdom, some kind of basis in power is frequently recommended. Parents and teachers must, after all, put their foot down and clearly enforce the rules. If you are too "nice," that means you've lost your "power" to enforce.

On the one hand, it was my "job" to enforce the law. On the other hand, I didn't always agree with whatever the supposed law was. I didn't simply accept that whatever assignment the teacher left behind was automatically "what's best for the kids," for example. I had to walk a thin line between using my personal judgment, and not undermining other teachers, parents, and rules.

The sub's dilemma—and it can also be the teacher's dilemma, the parent's dilemma, and the principal's dilemma —had a lot to do with how I would approach the students despite being under pressure to act authoritarian, unbending, and sometimes, complicit in their misery.

We could call one choice "go along to get along." This choice presents the least personal risk. In the picture of its extreme, I will simply yell at students to do as they are told, because that is what is demanded of them. For authority's own sake, it is best to keep students passive and obedient. If they must do their work, no matter any other circumstances or considerations, I will simply do whatever it takes to get them to comply. I will get them quiet and on task. No trouble for me if an administrator walks in. I will probably be judged less harshly by another teacher whose vision of the classroom is one of order and simple business.

-Too tired? Too bad. Your work is due at the end of class. Do it now.

-Don't get the point of this assignment? I didn't ask for your opinion. It's worth twenty points.

-Don't know when you'll use algebra in life? Trust me, you will. Or you might. You are not allowed to question the school curriculum, you're just a kid.

-You hate sitting down in a chair all day? Sit down **now!**

-Stop talking. You have work to do. People don't talk to each other in the real world.

This choice, though, is not good for "the students," if our vision of education includes humane treatment, the ability for students to make many of their own decisions, and the goal for students to understand *why* things are important or unimportant. It is also not as good an approach for "learning" as it might seem to those who do not know much about learning, or those who have not thought a whole lot about the purpose of education. As I said before: "doing" is not the same as "learning," and "learning" is not the same as "meaningful learning."

The other extreme might be to sit there doing nothing. I did this occasionally; other subs do it too. We're not superhuman. It's a tough job, and takes a lot of energy that sometimes we don't have. It's not just physical energy, either, but mental and emotional energy, and the psyche to deal with everything the students will throw at you (hopefully not literally). This approach relegates the substitute teacher to "group babysitter." But that is somewhat misleading to say, because for the most part, the substitute teacher effect has already decided this. Due to the sub effect—which speaks of systemic deficiencies much more than individual deficiencies—the "do nothing" method of subbing is sometimes all that we can do. For those who say otherwise, we would have to ask why they are so ready to question and blame individuals, but not systems; and if they have tried the job themselves.

Our job then, like I said before, is to take attendance and prevent catastrophe. The part in the middle where the sub is supposed to enforce students "working," is where I found a space to be different.

My way was not to enforce the doing-of-the-worksheet. My way was to engage in discussion and ask questions. If students found the worksheet (or whatever) engaging, or worth doing for some reason—we could work on that, and I'd help them. Otherwise, we could try something else.

It's like the time when a group of students had an assignment left behind that began with: "define *rock*." I'm not going to yell at students for not wanting to do that. What happened, though, was that I engaged students in a humorous conversation about *minerals*, which eventually led to questions beyond the study of geology. Of course, I would also remind them the assignment is due. (But they know.)

We need to view education—and school—through a wider and more humane lens. If we're concerned with learning, then let's talk about how people learn better when they are active and interested rather than passive and obedient. If we're concerned with humane treatment, and we should be, then we must consider giving the students far more autonomy than they've been given.

Yes, even the autonomy to choose not to do everything and anything they have been commanded—as long as it is not harming others. Or to learn something else; to learn in a different way; to learn at a different time. This is how the "real world" works, and when it doesn't work this way in our professional world, it should, usually. And even when it shouldn't—we're talking about K-12 education. This is different than a medical professional who has chosen their career and is in the middle of surgery. Allowing students time and choice right now does not mean they will be unable to cope with important deadlines and procedures in the future. That is a fear, not a fact. We cannot base our teaching of children and teenagers around this somewhat imaginary prediction of the future workplace—a workplace that will change so much in the next five, ten, and twenty years—and a workplace that we should also try hard to change for the better, rather than perpetuate its worst parts.

When I originally wrote this chapter, it was very different. It was a collection of approximately fifteen anecdotes, telling some of my thoughts and experiences during my time as a substitute teacher. I decided to take these entries out of the book, and re-write the chapter. I may post them on my website at some point. But now, I will close this chapter with just one of the original stories, because I believe it best illustrates "the sub's dilemma"—and it shows something of what I mean when I say we must adopt a broader view of education, school, and childhood.

"A beautiful compromise"

I have faced many dilemmas as a substitute teacher. Indeed, that may be most of my job: to face dilemmas, and get everyone out okay. Most of the dilemmas, however, are not as big a deal as adults typically think. We frequently make mountains out of molehills, because we are scared that the molehills may become mountains. (FEAR=False Evidence/Expectations Assumed Real.)

In this scenario I am working at a school where I've been multiple times, so it's somewhat familiar. I am given the plans for a particular class: almost always something the students perceive as boring "busywork." Today I have a few "IB" classes, and a few non-IB classes. The teachers always tell me that the "IB kids" are "good" and will not give me "problems," and will do their "work." Not as true as they think—but like I said, it's not always a huge deal, either. It's not like they are having fight club.

Not usually, at least.

Oh, it's Halloween. The students really, really don't want to do their assignment today. I mean, it's almost always like that, but maybe even more like that today. They have different plans. Even if I were the meanest sub from the black lagoon, I don't think they would "do their work," much less care about it. You can scare someone, by the way, but that doesn't make them actually learn or give a damn.

One student goes to draw a Halloween character on the board. Very nice drawing! This student is an artist.

Another student joins. And another. They start drawing costumed characters, and putting word art all over the board.

Are they all artists??

Here is the dilemma: Do I "let" them do this? Do I make a persistent effort to stand against them? The activity is, after all, getting in the way of "their work." It is apparently my job to make them do their work. I am the boss, and they are the contracted employees.

Maybe Halloween is different, but in general, I know exactly how most administrators, teachers, and substitute teachers in our current system would handle this situation. They would make the students stop. They would make the students sit down. They would make the students do their work. Or at least, they'd try.

Here is the ugliness of our system. It does not value who the students truly are, what they care about, or even that there are different ways to learn. It does not value beauty and expression. It does not value joy. It will actively work against the creativity and brilliance of youth and the natural spontaneity of humans. It fights against the idea that inspiration is one of the best precursors to action, and replaces the authentic motive of "inspiration" with the far lesser, and often oppressive, motive of "compulsion."

Teachers do generally value the more beautiful and humane virtues, yes. But in order to do "their jobs," they must regularly suspend or expel these notions. To me, that says our conception of what it means to be a classroom teacher, or a "sub"—or an adult—is way off.

I let the students draw on the board all day. It was fun, and their art was beautiful. They were learning in a different kind of way. They were being human on Halloween.

Maybe there's more to life and learning than what "school" typically allows. The substitute teacher effect happens because now, for a moment, they can catch up on being human... in an inhumane system.

Part II

The Psychology of
The Substitute Teacher Effect

3. Self-determination, Ethics, and Maslow

A few concepts from psychology and philosophy can give us a framework for understanding why the students think and act in the ways they do. These concepts can also help us to develop better goals and methods for our schools and social systems.

Self-determination

There are two definitions of "self-determination" in the Merriam-Webster online dictionary. One definition has to do with "the right of the people of a particular place to choose the form of government they will have." In other words, we want the United States of America to be able to govern itself. That's surely an important idea, but it's a bit irrelevant to our topic. The other definition is what we're after, and it is similar in that we want to "govern ourselves"—but it is more nuanced because it is an entire body of knowledge in the social sciences which involves individual humans rather than nation-states. The dictionary presents this second definition as: "free choice of one's own acts or states without external compulsion."

What does this mean? If we wanted people to be *self-determined*, it means that we want people to be able to reliably make decisions without outside interference. One way to think of it is simply "freedom," or individual liberty. It involves not only the freedom to make certain actions (behaviors), but the freedom to be happy, sad, or amused. And these actions, thoughts, and feelings originate in a particular individual's own sense of self—they are not forced from the outside.

This is not to say that every action is morally fine. It's to say that we want people to feel they are capable of making personal choices—and that they can do so without too much difficulty.

In philosophy, freedom can be a tricky concept, but we don't have to go so far in debating it. The truth is that everyone acts on the belief that freedom is real and that it is generally a good thing. We don't want to be locked up. We don't want to be controlled verbally, or abused psychologically. We want to be free to have feelings, and express them. We want to think for ourselves.

We want this not only for ourselves, but for our students and our children. And if we are not hypocrites, we generally want this for all people who are not a direct threat to the safety of others.

Unfortunately, our schools, classrooms, workplaces, and many other social constructs are designed—either deliberately, through negligence, or by accident—to oppress and suppress the individual's ability to act, think, and feel freely.

The scientific theory of self-determination goes beyond the dictionary definition. It is an entire sub-genre of psychology, and we can learn more about this concept if we go to the website *http://selfdeterminationtheory.org*. The first thing you would find upon visiting this website is the following statement:

"Self-Determination Theory is a theory of motivation.
It is concerned with supporting our natural or intrinsic tendencies to behave in effective and healthy ways."

We can see in this definition a critical addition to the dictionary definition. The dictionary basically said self-determination is individual freedom to make choices. But this more nuanced definition, which is more representative of the scientific theory, says something about "effective and healthy ways." It is not only the ability to think, feel, and act without real or perceived compulsion. It is the ability to do all that *in effective and healthy ways.*

Now, what those effective and healthy ways actually *are*, in specificity, will always be up for debate—and a matter of context. But the point is that we would like to preserve and support an individual sense of freedom, not only for its own sake, but so that this person can be healthy and meet their goals.

How does this apply to education, school, and society? My first introduction to this concept was several years ago, when I was watching education-related videos on YouTube. In this video, the speaker was talking about the ways in which the *very design* of school undermines self-determination—school actually undermines the ability of individuals to develop a sense of free choice that would be "effective and healthy."[1] Within self-determination theory, there are three "prerequisites," we might call it, to developing this ability to freely make choices that will be effective and healthy. This theory states that in order for a person to develop this ability of "self-determination," the person must first experience a sense of:

1. autonomy,
2. competence, and
3. relatedness.

Autonomy is a sense of personal control, that you believe you can control your own actions and environment. **Competence** is a sense that you are "smart enough" to navigate through life, or some particular situation. **Relatedness** is the sense that you are a part of something more than yourself—that you can "relate" to others in some personally meaningful way.

Now, consider the following:

> "SDT proposes that the degree to which any of these three psychological needs is unsupported or thwarted within a social context will have a robust detrimental impact on wellness in that setting."

Basically what is being said by this "self-determination theory" is that if you do not feel like you are smart enough, in control enough, and can relate to others, it is much more difficult (and much less likely) for you to "make your own healthy and effective choices" on a consistent basis.

It makes perfect sense, at least to me. Imagine someone who doesn't think they are intelligent enough, in control of their own life, or that they're some kind of alien. This person is likely going to be self-destructive, to whatever degree, and maybe even destructive to others—even if not on purpose. This person has a "void" in their own sense of self, and will likely struggle with personal freedom as well as consistently making "healthy and effective" choices.

It's not one or the other: either you feel autonomous or don't, feel smart or don't, feel a sense of relatedness or don't. The model would look more like a sliding, multi-dimensional scale—and since we are humans, there would be exceptions. For example, perhaps there does exist a person who strongly lacks a sense of autonomy, competence, and relatedness—and yet feels free, and is capable of consistently making healthy and effective choices. But it seems much less likely, doesn't it? It's certainly not a place where we should set our goals.

In the previous chapters, I briefly mentioned how schools (as well as other institutions and general cultural values) can undermine students' health and motivation. In upcoming chapters, I write about specific things we do in schools, classrooms, and general society, that thwart and destroy human health and motivation.

The most important part of this discussion is that these policies and practices, which stunt our growth and hurt us, **can be changed.** And they *should* be changed—to policies and practices that *support*, rather than *undermine*, the health and motivation of all students and citizens. Remember, this is not only more respectful and humane, it will even get people to learn and behave better. There is no downside except for the difficulty in shifting our efforts and priorities.

Ethics

It is not enough to think of "the individual." We live in a world of billions of people, as well as non-human creatures and a complex natural habitat. It is not enough to say "I do what is best for myself." We must encourage and support the ability of people to think of others and empathize with others. This is the deeper meaning of **ethics**, and without it, society breaks down.

Ethics is not religion, doctrine, or dogma. My preferred definition of *ethics* is the first sentence of its Wikipedia entry:

> "Ethics or moral philosophy is the branch of philosophy that involves systematizing, defending, and recommending concepts of right and wrong conduct."

Let's take a simple example. Is it wrong to kill other people? The vast majority of humans would agree that yes, it is wrong; at least under most circumstances. Where does this belief come from? If it originates or is contained within religion, doctrine, and dogma, then why do so many atheists and agnostics also believe it to be true? Sure, religious people can have ethics and ethical systems, but it is not required to be religious in order to pursue and subscribe to ethics. This is important, because it means there is no reason for ethics to be missing from our public school system. It's neither religious nor politically partisan. It is simply humane and responsible.

"Ethics" is ultimately a philosophical discussion between social participants, regarding the rights, wrongs, and rules of a society. It includes pacts between countries all the way down to personal interactions. It even involves beliefs and actions between humans and non-humans. It doesn't matter if you are religious or not: if you have a good ethical sense, you will avoid smashing beehives or dumping toxic waste into the ocean. Basically, you won't be an asshole.

Without a *deliberate* and *systematic* effort to discuss ethical dilemmas and considerations—life will be worse for all of us, and society will not last.

It's common sense... except that we are not doing it. Look at school and tell me what students learn from it, and within it, ethically speaking. What do they learn—both through the curriculum, **as well as** from general procedures, and the way people interact with each other?

We don't have ethics courses, for starters. In Finland, it is part of their regular curriculum. Not here.

Rules and procedures are generally not open for debate. Students are not really allowed to disagree with teachers, staff, administrators; kids are generally seen as inferior, automatically, if they have a disagreement with an adult. There is rarely discussion of who is right or wrong.

Built into the curriculum, school operations, and our system of evaluation, is the idea that a hierarchy determines what is right and wrong. If you disagree with the agenda and inflexible rules and procedures, you are simply wrong.

When students have disagreements with each other, they do not work it out. We encourage them to appeal to *us*.

We do not seem to care much about who is actually right or wrong, philosophically speaking. Even if we individually value ethics and responsibility—as teachers—much higher on our agenda *in actual practice* is **obedience**.

It may seem that ethics and obedience are similar, or that they overlap in many places. But far from being alike, they are closer to opposites. Obedience is all about accepting an externally imposed set of rules, regulations, procedures, and truths, no matter what they are. Ethics, rather, is about determining it together—and then making our life decisions in ways that go beyond the benefit of ourselves.

Imagine this scenario, which is very much our social reality. You're a student, and you are told you must follow the rules at all times. If you don't, you will face punishment/ consequences. By the same token, if you *do* follow the rules, you will receive a reward/award.

Is this student ethical, or are they obedient? Do they truly understand right and wrong, as it relates to the group—or are they thinking and acting purely for the benefit of *themselves?*

It was a rhetorical question. Our system of obedience trains people to *accept,* not to develop sophisticated judgment. The substitute teacher walks into the room. The students are more rude to the substitute teacher than usual.

Why? Because they are much less scared of consequences, and less likely to get in trouble. Not only are they potentially mischievous to the substitute teacher, they are more difficult toward their peers—because they are less likely to get a personal punishment/consequence. They can afford to be meaner; not because it is ethically right, but because temporarily, they do not have to obey.

I understand the teacher's plight; we have to deal with thirty students at a time, and we must "get them up to academic standard"—and so, we do not have "the time" to go through such things as "ethical dilemmas," and we do not have time to discuss things like "who is *actually* right or wrong." We've got to get to the next page in our lesson book. We have to assume "someone else" will take care of it.

But exactly what I'm saying is that this is the wrong set of priorities. We cannot sacrifice ethics to "academics," and we do not need to. Education cannot simply be about getting the class quiet enough for the teacher to direct an activity. It has to develop *whole people,* not just repeaters of facts and skills who have no idea how to treat each other, or why they are doing certain things in the first place.

Our emphasis on obedience in schools, the workplace, and our general culture, gets in the way of people developing a sophisticated sense of right and wrong. We must make room in the schools for the teaching and learning of ethics—not only in one course per four years, but in our general mode of operations within every class, within the hallway, within the lunch room, and even in the disciplinary office. (*Especially* there.) We need people to think for themselves. We cannot do that if we are constantly telling them exactly what to do, when, and why—and that they will be punished if they do not comply. We must encourage students to ask questions, debate dilemmas, and challenge authority, rather than tell them to simply be quiet and accept the rules that have been already laid out.

Aristotle once said: "education without the heart is no education at all." Authority can not be the reason for doing or not doing. We must educate both the heart and the mind together.

What "Maslow" Can Teach Us

Let's not forget about the physical body, or any other aspect of a person. The study of psychology is largely the study of what "needs" and "traits" people have—and then, depending on who you ask, how we can better fulfil those needs to heal and improve peoples' traits.

Just as schooling must, to a large extent, include the ability to be free, make choices, and have sophisticated group judgment—it must not forget that we are tied to our bodies. School must be *structurally designed* to support the physical health of students. If it is not, we will see problems in the mind, psyche, emotions—all of our aspects.

If we are hungry, we won't learn or behave as well. Simple enough, right? And yet, systematically, our schools are designed so that it doesn't really matter how hungry, sleepy, lonely, athletic, or different you are. If you are behaving "badly," you are probably going to get in trouble, yelled at, and maybe even thrown out. Best case, you will be uncomfortable. Academically, you are going to be judged more harshly: your "grades," which determine your future, in one way or another, will reflect and amplify (in one way or another) any problems that are beyond your control. In the idea of a grade or class rank is the idea that everything is up to you, and that someone else will rather arbitrarily decide who is better and worse. Please don't tell me that the "troubled" kids receive equal treatment, either academically or personally. We know this is not true. The more hungry, sleepy, disinterested, unloved, you are—the worse of a "student" they are going to say you are. I've heard teachers frequently referring to individuals and groups of students as "bad" kids. These teachers may otherwise be caring, but they have gotten in the habit of judging students by how easy they are to manage, and how willing they are to accept the teacher's own plan and personal joys. It's not easy to be a good teacher, or a good person. But one thing we must work to overcome is this personal judgement and labelling of students according to how well they follow the plan of the institution.

Maslow's "hierarchy of needs" is relatively familiar among educators, caretakers, and some parents. It has been expressed in the form of a pyramid, with five general "levels" of "needs." On the base of the pyramid we have needs which are more *urgent* (not necessarily more *important*). The general idea is that the lower levels must be "fulfilled" before we can/should consistently and reliably focus on the next level. The levels of "urgency" are:

1. Physiological
2. Safety
3. Love/belonging
4. Esteem
5. Self-actualization

I ordered these levels for writing purposes, but visually, they would appear in the opposite order: with the physiological needs at the base of the pyramid. In other words, physiological needs are the most urgent; then safety, love/belonging, esteem, and actualization.

Implications of "Maslow" for schools, classrooms, and systems

What this pyramid says to me, in summary, is that we must take care of the body and psyche *before* we focus on the intellect; and then, make sure the body and psyche are not undermined by/during our efforts to develop the intellect. Consider student "Adam." He has all these needs—as in theory, and perhaps reality, everyone does. He needs food, water, and motion (level #1—physiological); a sense of safety (level #2—safety); love and care (level #3—love/belonging); a sense of belief in himself (level #4—esteem); and finally, to be all that he can be in life (level #5—self-actualization). What this theory would strongly imply (and perhaps, what common sense should say) is that if Adam is hungry or sleepy, or feels unloved or unconfident, he is not going to reach his intellectual and personal potential (the top need, or "self-actualization"). Logically, to expect "the best" from Adam when he is physiologically and/or psychologically deficient, is not only unfair but foolish.

What are students *expected* to do in the classroom? They are all expected to try their best, mentally, even though most of them will have physical and psychological deficiencies. What happens in the end is that students will be punished and rewarded based largely on how hungry, sleepy, bored, or loved they are. Please don't tell me that's fair or wise.

If we want students to reach their potential, as well as to be healthy and feel respected, then in the long-term we must do nothing less than re-design both school and society.

Social efforts must focus on supplying food, housing, healthcare, clean water, and dignity—to all communities. By doing this, we will not only improve society, but we will improve the ability for schools to work with students.

Schooling efforts must involve a re-design of the entire system of teaching and learning in classrooms and school buildings. If we took Maslow seriously, we'd quickly see that schools and education programs are not designed with health and well-being as high priorities. They are designed to ignore, and even sacrifice, physical and psychological needs. Students are constantly sitting, listening, and unable to choose what they are doing, with no regard to their personal and physical feelings. This is a disaster for physical and psychological health.

To solve this problem, we have to start thinking about what is best for students *overall*—not just in terms of reading, writing, memorizing, and working with numbers—

and we can acknowledge what is better for them overall will be better for their intellect, too. Some solutions will require more funding, which means a greater social obligation to education and social equity. But some solutions will not cost a dime, and some will cost less than what we're currently paying. These will simply require a commitment to considering new ideas, and then changing how we do things.

On the small scale, and in the short term

Teachers cannot wave a magic wand, and suddenly, the school will have new programs and structures to support physiological and psychological health. The teacher often must play with "the cards that have been dealt." The teacher has a classroom and a curriculum, some degree of which has been passed down by political, administrative, and department directives. The teacher is limited in his or her response to poor health and well-being of students, and to the lack of opportunities that exist for supporting and strengthening their health and well-being. But I am fully confident that the teacher can change many things about his or her own approach. My own experience is enough evidence for me to believe this. It is not easy, but if you care deeply about your students, it is completely possible to modify your own methods in the classroom to support ideas like "Maslow," or at least do less damage than you would otherwise.

First, do not yell, threaten, or punish. This may be difficult to some teachers, staff, and administrators, since it is the norm in some ways. Even if we do not want to hurt students, and even for those who do not yell at them, it is much more difficult to not threaten and punish. Our adult culture is convinced that these should be a part of our procedure. Threats and punishments include "consequences," by the way—they are the same thing. I told you, it will be difficult for many adults.

But do not tell me it is impossible to avoid threatening and punishing, when I have done just that thing for the vast majority of my career so far. As a substitute teacher who does not have the benefit of familiarity with the students, I made a pact to not yell, threaten, or punish—and since then, I've kept it, with few exceptions.

Yes, I allowed myself to make mistakes, and I made rare exceptions when confronted with safety concerns and extreme levels of disorder. No, I would not allow myself to make "threats and punishments" a systematic part of my approach.

Did I have all the same obligations as a "regular" teacher? No, but again, I began every new day with the disadvantage of unfamiliarity, as well as being expected to enforce *someone else's* assignment. I promise you this: as a regular teacher, I will set the same standards for myself. No, I will not yell, threaten, or punish students when it would inevitably—in some way—be yelling, threatening, and punishing students for a lack of physical and psychological fulfilment. It is, at least in some way, not their fault. I am not going to make it all their fault, or act as if it is their fault.

Requests, yes. Respect, yes. Reasons, yes.

Yelling, threats, and punishments, no.

Ultimately, I believe the students become far more responsive under this approach, especially if you have the benefit of long-term familiarity, your requests are reasonable, and you make the class enjoyable to them. In my experience of working with them, observing other teachers' classes, and even asking the students questions about this issue—they are ultimately going to respect you more, and work with you more, if you do not yell, threaten, or punish. And it's simply having respect and good treatment of people.

The previous point covers a lot of ground: it requires tons of tolerance, patience, and empathy. **It also means** that you will not deny students basic choices like "going to the bathroom." Even at the risk of a student skipping out on class, you must not go down the slippery path where you barter with their bathroom rights. You must have tolerance for anything approaching basic human rights, such as eating, going to the bathroom, or even sleeping when exhausted.

And if you must deny an action, like eating in class, or talking to a friend—you must make your justifications clear, and deny with respect and reason, not anger. Oh, and the less a student dislikes you and your class, the less they will want to run away down the hall. So there's that.

Whatever power you have to alter the evaluation process, you must use that power in their benefit. I may speak heresy now, but my hope is that in a few decades the majority of teachers will at least not be startled when I say that **grades** are inherently harmful. My case against grades will be delivered at book-length, and until then, found in fragments throughout my writing. Alfie Kohn debunks the practice in his own work, which reviews large segments of educational psychology research. I strongly recommend reading this; see citation.[2] You should grade as little as possible, and whenever you can allow students to make the final evaluation, you should.

Speaking of which, you should give students as much choice as possible. This may involve asking them when to have a test: friday, or sometime next week. It may involve asking them to collectively decide on a due date, if there must be one. It may involve finding strategic ways of asking them what they wish to study, if you as teacher-under-mandate have any say in the matter. Pass down any choice you can to them. I will be writing more extensively about this process in future books; I will illustrate how I'd give students choice within the curriculum that they helped to shape. I even did it as a long-term sub, in the small spaces I was given to do my own thing. Few things will be more important for treating them fairly and getting them engaged. It is totally possible, even in a world that dictates everything to you, the teacher. Figure out a way. You are the one teaching them. You can decide, to a very large if not complete extent, how you will be treating and teaching them. Not only will this better treatment of students minimize, or eliminate, "the substitute teacher effect"—it will be one part of reversing all the significant problems that cause it in the first place.

Chapter 4: School's (Flawed) Design

How do we design school so that it works better for students? First, we'd have to know what is wrong. This chapter will examine our typical concept of "school," and unearth more of its problematic structures.

In order to know what is wrong, we will have to think about what it is like to be a student every day. Of course! To positively change the experience for students, we should first understand how they are experiencing it. What do we do that undermines students' ability to be healthy and interested in school—as well as respectful of themselves and others?

My analysis of school's structures will be presented in light of how they undermine physiological and psychological health, as well as ethical development.

Against "Autonomy"

Feeling a sense of autonomy (free will/choice) is one general element of "self-determination" (being in control of your own life and being consistently able to make good choices). However, in school:

Students have little or no choice in *what* they learn
Though they can occasionally choose an elective class (depending on how privileged their school and community is), the actual curriculum is pre-fabricated by default.

Students have little or no choice in *why* they learn
Social and economic agendas, as well as pseudo-motivational practices like grading, turn school into a quest to amass credentials, build a resume, and prepare for a hypothetical job—rather than "to learn what you enjoy, and for its own sake."

Students have little or no choice in *how* they learn

They must learn on certain timetables: students must do their "work" during class, if/when demanded, and they have little to no say in deadlines.

Teachers typically do all the "teaching"—as opposed to allowing students enough opportunity to learn from their own methods and sources, and from each other.

Teachers often omit or under-utilize various teaching mediums, such as visual or kinesthetic. People learn better when we use combined visual, auditory, and kinesthetic methods, as well as when we are active generally. The more the teacher is only lecturing, and the students sitting and listening, the less the students are learning—both quantitatively and qualitatively.

Students do not decide who will be in their school lives

They generally do not decide who their teachers will be, who will be in their classes, who will be next to their lockers, and so on. Sometimes, they may not decide who they can sit next to, or talk to.

Students do not decide their schedule

They do not decide how many classes they will take, at what times they will study during the day (many people do better in the morning, with an afternoon break, for example); nor do they decide when they will begin and end their day.

Students are rarely allowed to evaluate themselves

And if they are, it is never the final word.

The teachers, as well as the business/political system (standardized tests), will tell them how good they are (or aren't). Other people will tell them what they are good at (or not good at). The students internalize these foreign evaluations of themselves, rather than learning how to properly evaluate themselves and their peers.

Students must get permission to go anywhere

You cannot go to the bathroom unless you're approved. You cannot go through the halls unless you have a physical passport. Anytime you want to go somewhere other than your seat, you must consult authority.

Students must be unconditionally respectful

Adults are allowed to be rude, but students aren't. If they "choose" to disagree or "have an attitude," they are going to be punished or ostracized. How often is a student allowed to say "no" to an adult? The choice is not a real one—there is only one logical choice most of the time you disagree with an adult, and that choice is to obey—or suffer the arbitrarily imposed "consequences."

You can't even learn while standing up or lying down

As perhaps we could in "the real world."

Students are subject to security checks

Students must wear an ID, and sometimes, go through a metal detector. Perhaps this is for safety and legal reasons, but that doesn't take away from the point that it deprives them of yet one more bit of freedom; and there could be another way to go about the need for security and legality.

Students cannot choose their clothes, in some schools

Scratch one more choice off the list. Some students must wear "uniforms" so that they cannot even choose what they wear. And by extension, they are not allowed to choose a part of their identity, and express themselves in a way that is meaningful to them.

Students do not choose the food they eat

Students' lunch, and sometimes breakfast, is chosen for them. Sometimes, this is out of necessity. And yet it is still another choice they do not have, and another point for consideration.

The bottom line? Students' lives are written out for them; their daily choices prescribed by other people. It's almost as if they've been put on a conveyor belt. To suggest they have a good amount of autonomy in school would be laughable and impossible to defend. Do we really think this goes away after school is over? Or does it become a part of their character to know that they cannot choose things in life?

Against "Relatedness"

"Relatedness" is having the sense that you "fit in," "belong," or simply can "relate" to others in ways that are meaningful to you. Relatedness is really about *relationships*, in the broad sense of the word.

In school, relatedness is consistently struck down:

Talking is bad!

In many teachers' classrooms, students are not allowed to talk to each other, *almost ever*. Still, in the 21st century.

Talking is not bad, except for when it is

In other teachers' classrooms, students are allowed to talk to each other sometimes—but still not enough, if we're really concerned about emulating and preparing for "the real world." Talking to each other, and working with each other, is still thought of as "cheating" in many schools and classrooms, and by many educators, in circumstances where it should really be fine. Again, this is under the premise that educators so often invoke: that school must be like "the real world."

Students' classmates are randomized

High school students will have up to seven or eight different groups of people to be with, for short durations. They will not have much time during school to relate to their teachers, or any fellow student in particular. (This is one reason why they want to talk and laugh and play so much—they don't have enough chance to be around their friends.)

Schools and classes are too big

High schools are almost always larger than their elementary counterparts. Students will more naturally get lost, and become less known. Classes have thirty or more students. Many elementary schools are too large, as well. Most elementary classrooms are still too large. I would bet that if we asked teachers the single most important factor for improving their effectiveness, most of them would say "put less people in my classes." It might be the number one request, almost certainly in the top three. I think lots of students would ultimately agree.

Budget cuts means cutting social services

The following is from a CTU report, titled,
The Schools Chicago's Students Deserve.

"In Chicago, all elementary schools receive one counselor, regardless of enrollment, so schools with up to 1,200 students still have just one counselor. That caseload is almost five times the American School Counselors Association (ASCA) recommendation of 250. At the high school level, one counselor is assigned for every 360 students, about 1-1/2 times the recommendation. Much of a counselor's workday consists of coordinating test administration and paperwork, leaving her little time to actually counsel individual students or even small groups. No additional counselors are provided to schools in high poverty, high need areas; students' counseling needs have no impact on the number of counselors assigned to a school. There are currently 731 counselors working in CPS schools. Using the ASCA recommendation, there should be about 1,600."

(From the same report, employed psychologists and social workers are far under the recommended minimums of their professional organizations.)

Strictly business

Teachers and administrators, in order to be effective disciplinarians and task masters, often put up large walls between themselves and the students. After all, you can't be too nice and accommodating—so the thought goes—or you lose your power to maintain an "academic focus." Relationships are not only undermined by discipline and this kind of heavy "task focus"—but these priorities prevent relationships from ever forming in the first place.

Substitute teachers are fleeting, too

I subbed for an entire school district—and stayed at the same school for over a year. Tens of thousands of students seen; but I got to know very few of them. As for the rare exceptions, we still didn't have much chance to work with or speak to one another. By design, not choice.

Against "Competence"

Feeling an overall sense of "competence" means that a student would feel they are intelligent [enough] to take on any particular task, or intelligent enough in general. Essentially, to feel they are not "failures" by nature.

We tell students they are idiots all the time—just not directly. We sort them into winners and losers, "smart kids" and "not smart kids," "good kids" and "bad kids." Some of the ways we do this are:

Tests

Even before we get talking about *evaluation*—whether students scored high or low, or passed or failed—the very strategy of everyone taking the same test will affect students' psyches. (Mostly for the worse.) Some students will naturally be better at the tests, some won't be as good. They don't even need letter grades or points to determine this. Simply getting through a test with ease—or getting through it with some trouble—or not getting through it at all—will let them know immediately how "competent" they are. The good test takers will think better of themselves—often falsely—and the worse test takers will begin to believe they are stupid when the test is more difficult for them than it is for other people. Consider "the test" as students perceive them in schools: We have told them that these tests are the final barometer, or gatekeeper, of what they know; these tests determine if they can move on, or must stay; these tests know if the student has "passed" or "failed."

People come to see their test results in school as reflections of their own competence, despite that tests do not sum up or accurately describe anyone's competence.

Grades and points

Then we seal the deal. We confirm their stupidity with an arrogant statement of "fact": our strategy of grading, subjective though it really is, lets students directly see "the truth" of who is "better" and who is "worse." This is bad enough when students compare letter grades—but grading on a 100-point scale, as virtually every school and teacher does, allows students to develop their judgments of themselves and each other based on trivialities. Are you really 'not as smart' as the person who made 5 points more than you on the test—or is the truth more likely that the person with the higher grade recalled one more piece of trivia than you did? The students do not easily differentiate on this, especially since we constantly imply the former.

GPA is similarly destructive as the 100-point scale, because then we get into hundredths of a decimal place (3.51 is better even than 3.45)—still allowing us to judge each other based on trivialities. And being the culmination of all your grades, GPA is supposedly more important than a single class grade, which therefore tells us how "good" of a student/learner/person we are in the game of school and life. GPA is an illusory stamp of relative failure and success, which students internalize for the worse. It has great power to make students feel more or less competent than others—under a false pretense.

Ranks

Here is another way for students to build a false sense of their self-worth, and look down (or up) on others based on what is mostly arbitrary: rank them against each other based on these illusory letters and numbers. Again, they consistently come to believe this stamp is defining, and that's the most harmful part. This is what people eventually come to believe about intelligence: "smartness" is a linear scale, and there are people who simply have more than you, and people who have less than you. This is a false idea that social and cognitive scientists have left behind, and they left it behind decades ago. But much of our society still seems to believe it. Perhaps because school, at all levels, perpetuates the notion.

Tracking

We have *special ed* students, who are labeled less "smart" than students in "regular" classes—but wait, the regular students are not as "good" as the *honors* students—who are not as competent as the *AP* or *IB students* (I'm not quite sure which one of these is supposedly "smarter" or "better").

Tracking is not the best way to design schools. Though there is strong evidence against "tracking" in the educational research literature,[3] we do it anyways. Why? Because of our insatiable urge to sort students into piles of better and worse? One of the most solid truths I have learned about school is that students come to define themselves academically, and personally, based on their track, or even just the name of some class they're in. You're in AP Math? Smart!! You're IB? Good kid!! Anything else? Get ready to be inferior in life.

We as teachers, and some of our society, want to move beyond this horrible type of discrimination and false segregation—but we still endorse these kind of class and track divisions? Of course, it's not always up to us, but are we making an effort to overturn and replace these ideas?

Awards

This goes in the same group as tracks, grades, and points. Though we often give them in good will, they still send a subtle (and sometimes not-so-subtle) message to everyone else who didn't receive the award that they are not good enough, not smart enough, not capable enough. Of course, if you were, you would have won.

The damage doesn't end there. In school, we often use awards as extrinsic motivators, and extrinsic motivation tends to undermine the development of true intellect. They also perpetuate conditional feelings of competence: People who achieve things in life primarily to satisfy external demands will never be truly happy or confident. Nor will they be learning under the powerful influence of intrinsic motivation.

Award ceremonies on their own might not be so bad, but I'd say it's malpractice to use awards to entice and control students. Judging and sorting out of a "pure" intention is still questionable, and not automatically a good thing.

Wall charts

When we put those points, grades, compliments, and gold ribbons on the wall, now *everyone* can see—whenever they want—how only a few people are smart enough or good enough. Now it is indisputable who is which. We further solidify their false and destructive images: their view of themselves as competent or incompetent develops as contingent on temporary, external conditions, rather than an internal and reasoned feeling of worth. Peer pressure makes sure to harden the specious judgment, and leave little room for rebuttal or escape.

Evaluations in general

Any time we make strong personal judgments, we run the risk of inflating egos, harming self-images, and alienating everyone else who overhears or oversees. When we understand this, at first it may seem like we are now walking on eggshells. But as I learned, it is not as difficult as it initially seems (though it takes awareness and practice) to speak in terms of *informational feedback,* rather than words that the students will perceive as *punishments or rewards.* In a follow-up book, I plan to give some practical guidelines and specific examples for implementing this principle.

I included this point because teachers are trained to evaluate constantly, but not nearly as much to understand and be mindful of the psychological effects of their constant evaluating.

Unfortunately, we tell students they are failures all the time. We regularly tell them—usually indirectly—that they are not good enough for us, and not smart enough for the world. With the way school is designed, all it takes for them to experience this is *to be a student.* Even if we have good intentions—unless we are a radical exception, who is aware of all these issues, and consciously revolting against the norm—and consistently practicing new solutions—we will make many of the students feel incompetent in some way. Even if our practices and policies are not all our own choice, it will still happen to them while we work.

And even the best of educators only see the students for a small amount of time. This is what it means for school itself to be developmentally inappropriate; for the system itself to be damaging. With these kinds of structures, it is practically inevitable that the students will be harmed in major ways—despite if you improve yourself as an individual teacher.

Are there ways to help students understand what they have accomplished, as well as know their strengths and weaknesses, without resorting to these false evaluations and public humiliations? Absolutely! You don't have to make someone's worth contingent on another person's failure, or someone's else's arbitrary numeric judgment, in order to help them understand who they are and what they're good at. There are also ways we can help students understand that they are not so good at certain things, or certain things need improvement, without causing students to translate a feeling of failure or weakness into an entirely permanent and devastating character flaw. Evaluation can be constructive or destructive. I will discuss this more in future works.

Against "Judgment"

All of the above translates into a lack of opportunity to develop good judgment for one's own life, and a growing void of control over one's own destiny. Self-determination is stunted across the entire student population. Some individuals, of course, are more affected than others.

By the same token, if students do not have the time or proper opportunities to develop judgment for their own lives—it is just as likely that they will not develop good human judgment from a *group* perspective and for *everyone's* lives. This is **ethics,** and it is arguably a more sophisticated ability, and more difficult trait to develop, since you must go beyond yourself.

We often lose (or never properly develop) the ability to judge for ourselves and for others: What is right and wrong? Good and bad? The best choice for me, and the group?

It is determined *for* us. And to consistently determine it yourself, you must again be an exception to the rule. You must be working against "the machine" at all times, vigilant in every moment.

Structurally-designed apathy and illness

If we wanted healthy people, good learners, and people who enjoy what they are doing, schools would have to look, feel, and even sound differently than they currently do. The responsibility for a better kind of learner, and a better kind of person, does not rest solely on the schools and teachers—but it must include the schools and teachers. Ultimately, it's going to take a more informed and caring society, working together, to implement these changes.

5. Carrots and Sticks, Band-aids and Bricks (in the wall)

Part II of this book is titled "psychology of the substitute teacher effect." The substitute teacher effect is a student display of disinterest, inability to manage oneself/themselves, anxiety, desire for freedom, and a lack of caring—revealed when confronted with unfamiliar authority. This section has been a look at the policies, practices, and problems that underlie, create, and contribute to this response. This chapter in particular will be an examination of our beliefs and practices as educators—including at the classroom level, and all personal interactions—and how these policies, practices, and problems contribute to (or fail to rectify) student apathy and rebelliousness.

I believe that the vast majority of the time, it is not the teacher, administrator, or parent's actual intent to harm the student(s). Nevertheless, it is often what happens, despite our good intentions. It is built into the system: not just at the school and social level, but at the educator level.

The Teacher-Centered Classroom

Nearly a hundred years ago, John Dewey critiqued the many schools he observed:

> "*Traditional model is teacher-driven rather than learner-centered. Knowledge and skills are commodities to be delivered by the teacher to the student. Students are docile, passive receivers, while teachers are agents of this transmission of knowledge and skills.*"

If we pictured the school system as a tree, then the teacher-centered classroom would be one rotten root. Many of our policies and practices which generate student apathy and "misbehavior" flow from the concept that the role of the teacher is to pour their own pail of facts into the empty buckets of the students.

Students revolt. In the past, perhaps it was subtler. Now, it is more obvious. And the revolution shows no sign of slowing. In chapter eight, I say that we should embrace change and help to shape it, rather than fight the students. The teacher-centered classroom is a big reason for the students' rebellion. If John Dewey were alive today, he could make the same critique of our schools that he did in 1938.

Teacher "Survival" Strategies

(An inevitability of the teacher-centered classroom)

Even the phrase itself—so commonly used and accepted—implies a "battle" in which one side will lose at the expense of the other. Either the teacher survives, or the students survive. Something's got to give. Will it be the teacher's lesson and sanity? Or will it be the students' physical health (no moving or talking) and psychological health (no control over the content or procedure). This immediately points to a fundamentally flawed design of school and the classroom.

The most obvious structural flaw of our contemporary classroom—but far from the only one—is *large class size*. Though I pointed out in the last chapter that not all structures and procedures are out of the teacher's control, this one is predominantly decided by politics, budget, building architecture, and administration. Large class sizes, by their very nature of dividing the teachers' energy, attention, and focus, will require bad compromises. Something important will always have to give, and teachers will be focused as much (or more) on "surviving" rather than "teaching." Even teachers with good "classroom management" may not be aware of (or willing to admit) how much they are really compromising. They have been forced to focus on their own needs and procedures at the expense of what all the students are actually thinking, feeling, and learning. It is also what they've seen, what they know, and the way it's been for so long. Even the experienced, self-assured teachers may say they can "handle" a large class—but you may also get them to admit, eventually, that large classes are far less ideal for teaching, learning, and health.

Some of the most obviously conflicted "survival strategies" have been mentioned:

Shutting up the students. In worst cases, for the entire class period and most of the school day.

Keeping students in their seats. See above; as often happens for entire class periods, whole days, and whole years of school. It is generally an administrative expectation placed on teachers to keep students in their seats. (Which, if you ask me, is a prime example of how fundamentally poorly we are willing to treat children in order to preserve the system.)

Keeping students "on task." Educators frequently fall in line with this idea—whether it's out of survival instinct or because they actually believe students should, not even for a few moments, be allowed to think or do in a way that is unrelated to their assigned instructions. The very concept of keeping students "on task" reminds me of a ruthless factory supervisor who punishes the employees if they waste time on not producing as many widgets as possible.

This horrible idea of "time on task" is somewhat rooted in the structure of school, in which high school students must spend only 50 minutes per day with one teacher/subject. Naturally, the teacher will want to use all of their time "efficiently," before the factory bell rings and the students must go to their next shift. (The idea is also practiced regularly in elementary and middle schools. We can't blame all of this on high school. I have seen most of these problems when observing younger students, and within my own middle school student teaching experience.)

I'll critique this idea more in the future, but for now, the alternative to this idea of "keeping students on task" would include some combination of the following:

(1) More time with each teacher, less concern with specialized subjects

(2) Giving students tasks they value in the first place,

(3) Helping the students see otherwise uninteresting "tasks" as intrinsically valuable, and

(4) Actually allowing them to be humans with the right to decide how to use their own time—in other words, accepting a broader view of education, as previously illustrated.

These are not all of the changes that must take place, but they are some of the most important ones.

Borrowing from the same crazy edu-bucket where we found *on task,* schools (and teachers themselves) regularly endorse and employ a similarly Orwellian *"on track."* Do we listen to ourselves when we say these things? Schools actually use this phrase positively and unironically, as if there is some "track"—designed by others, of course—that students dare not venture from, or they will fall off and be lost. More factory imagery comes to mind. Highly advised not to be a creative person, because I guarantee your track won't match *theirs.* (Whomever they are.)

While I sympathize with the teacher, and understand the need for some kind of order, I also know that if the teacher must always be worried about his or her own survival—and the school obsessed with designing a student's life for him/her—that leaves less room to be concerned about student health, learning, and control over their own pursuits. These are not only problems caused by large classes, they are also problems rooted in the very idea that the teacher/school should always be control—the teacher/school is active and in charge, while the students must remain passive and simply "followers of the instructions." Once students are more involved in determining their own curriculum and environment, once students are more active with project-based learning, once students learn and practice *reasons* to respect the teacher (and each other)—these "survival strategies" become less necessary, if not pointless and counter-productive. When students are allowed to explore rather than just repeat and follow, there will be less need for the school to dictate their exact "track."

These are deeply embedded structural problems, and in the meantime, teachers will have to do their best to respect students while they are making compromises. Teachers, staff, and administrators will have to develop greater patience and empathy so that they can deal with the students over time, rather than opt for short-term "solutions" based on threats, bribes, punishments, and a personal taste for authority—which are harmful to the whole student, and in the long-term.

We must especially understand and acknowledge the harms of "behaviorist" management strategies. In our haste to use our time "efficiently," and keep an orderly classroom, it is normal for teachers to turn to "classroom management" methods that aim to fix the students' *action in this moment*—even at the expense of their physical, psychological, and ethical health—and their intrinsic motivation to learn.

Carrots and Sticks

You may have heard the phrase before. If you aren't sure what this refers to, it is a method for getting some animal to pull your passenger cart—or, you may be getting the horse to GO while you are sitting on the saddle. Maybe you're betting on your chosen animal to win a race. In any case, the stick is a painful enticement; the carrot is not physically painful, but a psychological manipulation that serves the passenger more than the animal.

The animal analogy is supposed to be illuminating. In many ways, we treat students like they are animals. In the human world, *carrots and sticks* is a reference to an overall philosophy of "motivation" (which some would say is based on an outdated psychological theory of *behaviorism*)—the fundamental idea that humans can be (or must be) controlled and enticed through punishments and "rewards."

Carrots and sticks is the inevitable strategy that will be used when school exists in its current form. It is how our teachers and schools operate on a fundamental level:

Fearing punishments

If you don't [action] you will [get in trouble].

If you don't [action] you will [lose future opportunities].

Promising goodies

If you do [action] you will be [rewarded with a grade].

If you do [action] you will be [rewarded with approval].

If you do [action] you will be [rewarded with .... stickers, praise, awards, parties, cake, gift certificates, etc.].

This is, by far, how we "motivate" students in school.

(The alternative? *Making the experience valuable to them, which involves letting them choose many of the things they value, and working **with** them to build a valuable curriculum and environment.*)

The alternative would be building an education system around *intrinsic motivation*—in other words, something much closer to the students' actual needs and desires. (More in chapter seven and future works, or see citation for more reading suggestions.)[4]

Band-aids
An Illustration via Three Analogies

For the students to not need "extrinsic" motivators is difficult to imagine—not because it is impossible, but because it is so far from where we are. We believe—if not in our hearts, then with our policy and practices—that "band-aids" are necessary. Maybe, we say, they are the only option.

Big Problem #1: Apathy and Misbehavior.

Common Solution: Classroom management.

Outcome: *Beach ball under water.*

Analogy: When you hold a beach ball under water, it stays under water temporarily. Meanwhile, the pressure builds up, and eventually it will be released. This is the substitute teacher effect. The students are no longer being held under water, and rise to the surface violently. Classroom management is the very idea that the students must be controlled by the teacher. In reality, the goal is not to delve into ethical dilemmas and come out with a better understanding of how and why to act. The goal of classroom management is to bend the students to the *institution's* reasons; these reasons generally disappear when the teacher disappears. It shouldn't be a surprise that they act out when they are no longer being held under water.

Pushing the beach ball under water may solve some problems for *the teacher,* while they must teach on their own class time—but it does not solve *the students'* problems in the long run, because it ignores and undermines self-determination and ethics. It actually creates a vicious cycle, in which a human will continue to feel ever more controlled, and next time may react even more violently in order to assert himself/herself.

Big Problem #2: Disobedience.

Common Solution: Discipline.

Outcome: *Slowing down around police cars.*

Analogy: Adults know what I'm talking about. Drive along the highway, and watch what happens when a police car is spotted on the side of the road. Everyone slows down. The adult drivers *were* technically disobeying—but now, for the moment, they must obey. What happens, though, right after we pass the police car on the side of the road? We start to speed up again, and arrive back to our original speed. It's fine if we don't get caught.

The most clear example of this phenomenon is *swear words*. Many students will stop swearing, or swear less, in the presence of teachers or parents. But if you walk around the school hallway, or encounter them in their natural habitat, you really didn't change a thing about them when you told them to stop saying bad words. They just stopped in your presence. Even if swearing is bad, we don't honestly talk to them about *why* it is considered bad. We just tell them to stop, and sometimes, they stop in our presence. It really changes nothing about them; they do not think about *why* swear words are bad (if they actually are).

Oh, and "police cars" themselves often drive over "the speed limit." How hypocritical, and *it must not actually be bad*. That's what we learn: not true right and wrong, but to be tactful and deceitful. That's how we learn: from observing actions, not just words.

We are lying to ourselves, playing a little game—and this was just one example. In a way, all of our calls for them to simply "behave" and "listen" and "have respect" in our presence are the same. We simply demand for a change in their action at this moment. If there's no dialogue, or mention of the reasons, it's a hasty appeal to *behaviorism*.

(The alternative would be integrating "ethics" and democratic modes of operation, lessons, and ventures into schooling itself—talking about these things and taking action to actually become more *ethical*, instead of simply expecting temporary behavioral changes in order to stay within the behavioral norms. Once again, this would include a re-evaluation of *what we're asking students to do*, and it would have to include them in the process. How can we reasonably expect them to "behave" after making them feel ignored?)

If you discipline students, especially without dialogue, you are not really changing their values or who they are. You are making them slow down when they are around perceived authority. The substitute teacher can see this phenomenon more clearly, because the substitute teacher is much less perceived as an authority—and thus, can easily observe the *"be bad if no consequence"* mode of thinking.

Big Problem #3: Students are not yet educated.

Common Solution: Strict, standardized instruction.

Outcome: *21st-century factory-workers-in-training. AKA widgets for the global economy.*

Analogy: Students can't read very well? Force them. Make it mandatory. Make it repetitive. Tell them exactly what to do; exactly how to do it. *Demand* that they learn. (Or simply, work.) Grade for participation. Set strict deadlines. Use sticks and carrots. Tell them that if they don't, they will fail in life. Take out the joy.

Now, since they are human, they hate school and hate to "learn."

No, it's not all the teacher's fault. I keep saying that it isn't. But the teacher is part of the system—sometimes, just another brick in the wall.

Bricks in the Wall

"The system is just all of the people."
(Angel L., high school student)

Flowing from the imperative to maintain order at all costs, and to follow precise instructions (often used interchangeably with "learning," though they are not the same)—we get the "rules" of school and the classroom environment. What do students often "get in trouble" for doing in the classroom? The answer is *being human:* talking, standing, moving, using their phone, being bored, being tired, being hungry, being sick, having a different opinion, having a certain preference, having a strong personality. Even if denying these things were somehow "necessary" in order for students to learn, (it's not, especially if we changed the structures and expectations), that doesn't make this phenomenon less true or less harmful. It only makes sense that we rethink a system which requires the frequent silencing of basic human thoughts, feelings, and actions.

Another Brick in the Wall is a song written by Roger Waters of the band Pink Floyd. It is a dark story of the U.K. boarding schools several decades ago, and the students' eventual rising up to overcome their mistreatment. While the antagonist teacher in the music video is more extreme than the typical teacher of modern day schools, the concept is still true that even despite their good intentions, teachers end up denying students opportunities and striking down their general humanity. We have a dilemma to face: how can we reconcile? Students are turned off of "learning" every day by the things we say and do, often under the reason that we "must" say and do those things in order to be classroom teachers in this system. We perpetuate "behaviorism" with our sticks and carrots. We patch up problems rather than solve them. The students come to see other people as rivals, the world as an obstacle course, and their own dreams as beside the point—all in order to "succeed." The students might even say to us: *Hey, teacher! Leave us kids alone.*

It is not even rare to hear them say things like this, and sometimes they are thinking it, even if they don't say it. Go spend some time in a high school, and you will hear them say this, too. By the way, I think the modern equivalent is: "you're doing too much."

What students ultimately learn

"We're not gonna change. You change."

If school were an entity, this would be its loudest statement. Break the rules? Too bad for you. After all—the rules, for some reason, cannot change. And guess what? That's what the world is like. You can't change the world.

You are not in control of your life. We are.

Just like we saw in chapter four—here you do not make your own decisions about what to do, how to do it, when to do it, or why to do it. We have made your choices;

you will fill the role that we have designed for you. And that's what it's like in "the real world." *They* will command you.

Why? Because I said so.

This is a bad reason for pretty much anything; a horrible justification for virtually any practice. But this strategy is grown in our culture and legitimized in our schools. If students don't like it or want to do it, they have to do it anyways.

Why? Again, simply because someone told you to. We will even say, often, that we do not need a better reason. This is a reflection of our social values, and our general approach to people with less power than us—especially those who are younger and more vulnerable.

It's for your own good.

Finally, the shaky rationalization that can be invoked for any possible command. Though it can occasionally be legitimate, at least as often it has been one of the most dangerous "justifications" adopted by humankind. By invoking this reason, you can invade countries, take away the rights of citizens, and physically hurt people.

Before this rationale is used, we must very carefully examine what our requests entail, and whether we are including students in the share of power. To say that everything we make them do is "for their own good," is either ignorant or a big lie.

We must constantly ask ourselves the question: How often, despite good intentions, are we contributing to the problem? We must make sure that we are inspirational guides and fair leaders to them, not obstacles. If the problems are too great for one person to change, then we unite for change. We stand up, and we change the system.

In fact, this is the only way.

6. Conflicted society,
Conflicted schools

What is "the system?" Though it includes our schools and classrooms, the system is much more than that. What we do in schools and classrooms is some kind of reflection of what we value culturally, and the general state of society.

Are we in good condition? Are we healthy? Are we democratic? Do we have control of our institutions? Do we value evidence and ethics?

In April 2015, in his small town of Burlington, Vermont, Bernie Sanders announced that he was running for president. At the time of this writing, Sanders has lost his unlikely race for the Democratic nomination, but his campaign spoke volumes about the state of our nation and world.

At the time of his announcement, Sanders was a virtual unknown, a local hero who had served as a public official for many years. This small-time, grumpy, frumpy old man went up against one of the most well-established and well-funded presidential candidates in American political history. He also came close enough to winning that, for a while, he was considered a viable candidate for the presidency. This self-described "Socialist," which was supposed to be a derogatory term, received more small donations to his campaign than any other presidential candidate in our nation's history.

How did he do this? I believe Bernie Sanders garnered so much support because he spoke honestly about the problems we face, articulated them clearly, and showed us the hope and possibility for solving these problems.

"These problems we face did not come down from the heavens. They are made by bad human decisions, and good human decisions can change them."

(Bernie Sanders)

The mother of all illnesses

As Bernie Sanders frequently reminded us throughout his campaign, our country faces an incredible amount of child poverty. Fifty-one percent of public school students—that's over half—are below the poverty line.[5] Not only should it be common sense that poverty negatively affects people, including students, in a drastic way—field and lab research has confirmed this over and over again.[6] Educators are expected to deal with the consequences of poor communities and childhood poverty, including violence, apathy, sickness, lack of basic necessities, and lack of educational opportunities in the home and community. Of course, this makes it more difficult to teach, inspire, and even just deal with students—who bring their issues and conflicts into the school and classroom every day.

It is not just the poor who are hurting. The middle class has been shrinking for decades. Wages stagnate, jobs outsourced, unions busted—there has been a slow movement to increase corporate profit at the expense of our general society's welfare.

The "upper-middle" class, and obviously the "one percent," will have their physiological needs met—going back to Maslow—but that doesn't mean they are truly confident or at peace. These groups are not immune to other kinds of illness. If you think physical malnourishment is the worst that could happen, try losing your mind, your purpose, your family, your friends—isolated by your wealth and way of life. Paranoia and depression are hardly "better" than hunger. Mental health, relationships, and values are a form of wealth that the so-called "wealthy" often lack, or lose.

For all the problems that had been articulated by Bernie Sanders—and I will spare you the statistical details, as you've probably heard Sanders' ranting by now—it's been explicitly said (and often implied) that "the mother of all illnesses" is our corrupt political system.

How can this be true? Well, if Bernie Sanders was right that these problems are born from bad human decisions, and good human decisions can solve them—and if it's correct that we are the richest nation in the history of the world (and it is correct)—then why are people still going hungry and homeless in such large numbers? Why are public schools and health clinics still struggling to stay open? Why are our roads still falling apart? Why are thousands of species quickly going into extinction, as scientists have come to the understanding that we under-predicted the already devastating threat of climate change?

(It's very much because the people making our big decisions are not making the right ones.)

It's good to ask, then, who are these people that are making most of the decisions which cause us to be sick and violent, keep us jobless, and stop us from addressing preventable catastrophe like *climate change*?

Just a few of the most powerful people

A now-famous study recently concluded that the vast majority of Americans have virtually zero effect on public policy.[7] The study also found that the top few percent of the wealthy have a higher chance that their wishes will be written into law; however, the ones who really determine the law are the big corporations, by way of their lobbyists. If you didn't know how a bill becomes a law, the wealthiest industries hire lobbyists and lobbying firms, who present model legislation to Congress, which then drafts and passes this legislation because their political campaigns are funded by the corps.[8]

This study concluded that we are not living in a "democracy." By definition, we actually live in an oligarchy: a handful of people own the government.

We have the power to write equity and prosperity into law. We have the power to distribute resources to those who need it, and give democratic control of institutions (such as public schools) to the communities who work, learn, and play in them. But we don't. Why not?

(A few people want it all.)

Even if that means us getting less and less, or none.

Bernie Sanders' quote about "man-made problems" was very similar to Nelson Mandela's declaration that *"poverty is no accident. Like slavery and apartheid, it is man-made and can be removed by the actions of human beings."* Sanders and Mandela shared a sentiment with Martin Luther King, Jr., who spoke these famous words: *"There is nothing new about poverty. What is new, however, is that we have the resources to get rid of it...."* and thus, *"the curse of poverty has no justification in this age."*

The massive power and wealth imbalance that exists, and the bad decisions and decision-makers which maintain poverty, are a major source of our problems. But, as with this book, I am interested in getting to the very bottom of things, whenever possible. So I ask myself: is this "corrupt political system" really the mother of all illnesses? If we had the right kind of government "of the people, by the people, and for the people," we could use our rules and resources to help more among us. Certainly, that would let us fix poverty, and everything else... including our schools.

Right?

What is the true source of our problems?

I don't think poverty, bad politics, or even greed are the deepest roots of our problems. These are the roots to many problems, and yes, we must fight and overcome them. I am actively doing it myself. But like the substitute teacher effect, I believe these are still *symptoms* of an even deeper problem. Even poverty, political corruption, and greed flow from something that is more fundamentally wrong.

The greatest problem of all may simply be our culture itself: what we believe, what we value, our way of life. And not just *our* culture, but pieces of ideology—ideas and concepts about how to live—which make their way into most modern cultures, and are socially destructive.

Underlying our power imbalance, for example, is an idea that it is fine for some people to have far more power than others, and be able to indiscriminately make the decisions that cause so much harm to others.

Underlying sexism, racism, classism, and all the other "-isms," is the idea that "other" humans are generally inferior to ourselves, based on certain traits that are different from our own. Sexism, racism, and classism are real, and their consequences are real, but what enables all of them is a faulty underlying belief which has to do with how we live and view the world. Sexism, racism, and classism are all different "brands" of the same bad approach to social life. They are all a branch of a certain underlying conception of "humanity," and how we must live individually and collectively. These ideas continue to exist, mostly in the subconscious, due to a lack of ethical sophistication and a failure to re-examine cultural assumptions.

Ideologically, I would say we are not an ethical society. Our bad ideas, or theories about how and why to live, lead to bad outcomes in social reality. Even if suddenly and magically, we all had enough food to eat—and everyone had a home, and lots of disposable income—our destructive cultural ideology would assure that some people end up losing their food, respect, and comfort. It would be inevitable, like filling a cup of water that had holes in it.

It would be inevitable because people would sabotage themselves, and if that didn't work well enough, we'd also sabotage each other. We'd rationalize to ourselves, in one way or another, that this is what it means to live. Even if we had money, we'd self-destruct (as a disproportionate amount of lottery winners seem to do). Even if we were not hungry, we would take other peoples' food, as the richest, most powerful among society have always made clear they are willing to do.

I am not a cynic. A cynic would say that this is inevitable to humanity, a fact of nature, the laws of the universe, and simply "life." I don't believe that. I am an optimist, overall—and I believe, supported by evidence and reason—that these ideas and conditions can be changed. It is only inevitable if we do not change our beliefs and our ways.

I would also say that what I just explained is the reason why systemic, lasting change only comes from the bottom-up, not the top-down. Our problems cannot simply be legislated away by political representatives. It requires mass movements—and will require massive efforts in education, both within and outside of the classroom.

If our beliefs and ways are to be changed, ethics education would be one necessity for overcoming flawed pieces of cultural ideology and replacing them with better ones. Making "ethics" an explicit part of "education" won't completely fix our problems, on its own, but it can and must be a big part of the solution. Without ethics education, I believe we are more likely doomed as a species. If we're not thinking about how and why to live, deliberately and systematically, we're hardly gonna come up with better ways to live. If we did, it might be too late.

The best time to do this (aside from "as soon as possible") is during the development of youth—the development of the next generation of people who will re-create our culture and society.

I used to blame individuals for their faults, but now I understand that not everyone can be an exception. Educators (not just teachers) must be at the forefront of an effort to make ethics, wisdom, compassion, food, and housing the rule. This will require a systemic re-evaluation and re-design. Otherwise, a conflicted society will make conflicted schools—and the substitute teacher effect, though a telling symptom, will be the least of our problems.

Part III

Is there a light?

7. The student-centered classroom

Few of my ideas are original. One of the benefits of being a substitute teacher for several years was that it gave me much more free time, and fewer responsibilities, than I would have as a regular classroom teacher. I spent a lot of this time researching. And it's not as if I spent several years reading books in a library, or hiding in some cave in the middle of nowhere, while I performed a cerebral exercise about education. As I read and researched, I was simultaneously in the schools—every day—asking questions to teachers, students, and staff, and doing my own practice. At the end of my student-teaching experience, I only had vague philosophical concepts about what we should do differently. But now I have a high degree of confidence in my ever-evolving ideas, which are based on years of reasoning, research, experience, and being challenged.

I am confident that one of the very best big ideas of all, in education, is *the student-centered classroom*. I will thoroughly explore this concept, especially in my next book—and of course, as a teacher. For now, I will give a summary.

Element #1 - Student interest actually matters

While we may say or think "student interest" really matters in the traditional classroom, it sure doesn't seem like it to the student. That's because in reality, it doesn't matter so much what interests the students have when the curriculum, procedures, "point values," and syllabus are already set in stone upon their arrival.

In the traditional classroom, and especially when the course was not chosen by the student, "relevance to the learner" is not a deliberate approach but often merely coincidental when it does occur. If the student has other things they would like to learn, those things will be a distraction from "the curriculum" and a nuisance to the teacher. Remember, you must be on task and on track. And as a student, you don't have much to do with the task or the track. If your personal interests are in conflict, as a student, then you are at a standoff with the class itself. The teacher is going to teach what is being taught. If you don't like it, it doesn't really matter who you are or what you would like to learn. You are expected to swallow whatever is thrown at you by the teacher, the state, or whoever else is part of the curriculum. Then, you are to spit it back out at test-time. Finally, you get your "grade" of how well you "performed."

In the student-centered classroom, however, relevance to the learner is the most valuable and essential guide. While the broad subject *may* be determined, such as "History"—and a theme *may* be pre-selected, such as "The Founding Fathers"—the collective student voice is valuable in determining what will be studied and how it will be studied. Teacher guidance and preferences are not off-limits, but they no longer dictate everything about the course.

Element #2 - "Democracy" is a verb, not lip-service

In the student-centered classroom, the students will (along with the teacher) **create their own classroom environment by developing their own classroom rules and procedures**. This would make some teachers uneasy, since it wouldn't seem to work if we were unfamiliar with the approach (and the methods for making it happen). But done well, this is a more educational and respectful approach. The teacher relinquishes his or her position as dictator, and becomes first among equals. The teacher is now "in control of putting the students in control." The teacher is still a leader—just not an unyielding autocrat. Teacher is guide; not micro-manager.

Contrast this with the typical classroom, in which the teacher is the sole authority who must always enforce the law (of which students had no part in contributing—again, perhaps an indication of the state of our "democracy"). This does not help students to develop ethically, socially, or in civics. The students, feeling little ownership of their own space and time, face the sharp choice to either obey or rebel. Whichever they choose in the teacher-centered classroom, their behaviors will more typically be *reactions*, rather than based on their own deep understandings of what is important (recall ethics and self-determination). We would always have to keep pushing the beach ball back under water, because we assumed that we needed to fight it directly.

John Dewey believed that schools should be "laboratories of democracy"—otherwise, how would we actually create and maintain a democratic society? "Democracy," however, is not what our schools are now. They are much better at modeling a totalitarian society.

Element #3 - Active students, not passive

In the student-centered classroom, teaching and learning is generally project-based. There is room for teacher instruction, and even the occasional lecture. However, "instruction" becomes less important than "guidance," and lecturing is now supplemental rather than fundamental. The students are much more active in teaching themselves and each other, rather than simply listening and following instructions every day. Worksheets and textbooks are rare—for the most part, replaced by "primary sources" and hands-on activity.

Element #4 - "Assessment" is a conversion, not a stupid game

Since school's primary purpose becomes "to help students grow personally, socially, and in civics" (that is currently its secondary purpose, behind *meeting the institution's needs)*—assessment becomes centered around *dialogue,* rather than existing for the purpose of inaccurately quantifying and sorting the students. This means the grading game is over—it no longer serves its purpose, as words and observable phenomena reign supreme in the land of evaluation, and intrinsic motivation beats out extrinsic motivation when the goal is to teach and learn what is more valued and valuable. The need to "rank and sort" takes a back seat to best practices for student development, as informed by educational research. I know, what a radical idea!

———

There are many other considerations and fundamentally different traits of the student-centered classroom. I am far from the first person to have these ideas; there exist tons of evidence, research, and experience to back up the student-centered classroom as not only a viable alternative, but a clearly *better* alternative.[9] I have one final point regarding "change" in general:

While schooling should be geared more toward the student's needs than the institution's needs, there are many challenges that will make this difficult. Of course! It is more difficult to actually care about each student, and do more precise things that help them, than expect all of them to conform to one model. The journey to a "student-centered" system of education will not be a "neat" process, nor will we necessarily reach our ideal. As with so many things in this shared world, there will have to be compromises, and there will be challenges along the way.

What makes it "worth it" is that we can make smaller and better compromises. Though change often requires struggle, the student-centered classroom remains possible and preferable. Take a look at the following simple illustration:

serves student <——————— . ———————- > **serves institution**

On the right side we'd have "institution-centered" schooling. As John Dewey said in the early 20th century: The center of gravity is outside the child. Students are passive recipients into which "facts" are "poured" by the teachers. The students are expected to bend to the institution's rules and policies, which are set. The rules, policies, and standards are the same for everyone. What matters most is that the students conform to outside expectations. "Proper knowledge and skills" are always defined by the authority, and the students are to "achieve" this set knowledge and skills. The students set out to copy a foreign model, which may or may not have anything to do with them personally. True creativity is difficult to come by, because the goal is not "to create" in the first place, but almost exclusively to re-create what someone else has already created.

By definition, this kind of schooling is impersonal, and at best, can only be "somewhat relevant." In our current paradigm, our schools generally fall in this range. While a certain class or teacher can be further left or right, it is more an exception than the rule, and the school system itself is within a hypothetical window, for example:

serves student < ——[—.————]- > **serves institution**

By contrast, we have the student-centered ideal, all the way on the left side of this scale. In this dream world at the furthest left point, school would perfectly cater to the exact needs and desires of every single student, while also serving a proper social and civic function.

This can probably never happen in its entirety, and it's not even a good idea to sacrifice all of "the institution's" needs (which must exist to some extent, or the students wouldn't have a place to go, or human teachers to teach them). But the institution should exist primarily to serve the students, rather than the other way around. If we did set our goals to the left—and then, followed through accordingly—we could one day wake up in a world where the range is more like the "diagram" on the following page:

serves student < -[———.—-]——-— > **serves institution**

We should take every opportunity to move that window over to the left. It is not *the institution* that is so important—nor is it ultimately so important what the teacher wants, as the students' lives are not rightfully the teachers' to determine.[10] While there is some room in public schooling for social expectations and responsibilities, as well as human personality and teacher preferences—the major reason for school's existence should be, in both word *and action*, one of empowering students so that they can better define their own learning experience—and thus, their societies and destinies.

8. Embracing the revolution
(of a generation)

"That there was need for the reaction, indeed for a revolt, seems to me unquestionable."
-John Dewey

    I believe in public education. I believe in teachers. I believe in parents. And I believe in people. But I do not believe in what we're doing right now. "The substitute teacher effect" is a sad reminder that we have a long way to go. The light at the end of the tunnel is not more obedience, persistence, grit, rigor, testing, or anything that implies more of the same. The light at the end of the tunnel is a completely new idea of schooling, and a new idea of who is responsible. (All of us.) But it can't simply be anything which is "different" than what we are doing now. Change must be driven by the desire to do better for a future generation. It must be *ethical* change: powered by the will to understand what is right and wrong, to come up with better alternatives, and then pursue them.

    In conversation, a student once told me: "If a teacher is gonna be lame, we're not gonna let them teach." The high schoolers don't always have the most sophisticated responses, but they do get straight to the point. This student was not simply saying that they want their class to be "all fun and games," as we sometimes accuse them of wanting. In the context of our conversation, and based on my conversations with students around the city, I felt this student was speaking more broadly about the "way" we are doing school. Why should students sit by, quietly, if their curiosity is not being piqued? If they don't believe it's really helping them?

The students are fighting for themselves, and for the future. And just because someone is a teacher by profession doesn't mean they're automatically helping.

Lerone Bennett Jr. warns:

> *"An educator in a system of oppression is either a revolutionary or an oppressor."*

Note the "either." Implied in this statement is the idea that we must choose one or the other.

In our "system" of oppression:

If you are not a revolutionary—you are an oppressor.

To not be an oppressor—you must be revolutionary.

Teachers must not be a part of this "system" that is working against the students. We can only stand *against* the oppression by standing *with* the students. We cannot "prepare" them for oppression by oppressing them. That makes us the bad ones.

This means that even while we work to transform "the system," and even before it is transformed, we must persist in finding ways to treat students respectfully and humanely. We must entertain their challenges, rather than reflexively deny challenges. We must help them challenge the structures of hierarchy, including our own power over them; and all policies and practices which are not useful, sensible, or fair.

We must not condemn them for factors which are largely out of their control.

We cannot simply be concerned with their "behavior"—with taking away their power, and turning them docile—as classroom management methods typically condone.

We should be more concerned with what those behaviors are trying to tell us in the first place.

Conclusion:

The Substitute Teacher Effect

So what is the substitute teacher effect, why does it happen, and how can it be prevented?

The long answer, of course, was this book.

The shortest answer I can give is that "school" is disconnected from what humans, especially younger humans, need and desire. "Society" is also disconnected from what is most humane. The substitute teacher effect is but one visibly damaged leaf that sprung from an unhealthy tree.

―-

The substitute teacher effect is what happens when students do not like what they are doing, and now have an opportunity to get away from it. Students frequently do not like school, because it is developmentally inappropriate—it fails to regard them as whole people with their own problems and interests. School is also irrelevant to their own lives—not in every single circumstance, but consistently, and in large part.

These are problems not only because it makes their lives "boring" and "difficult," (though that is important to consider), but also because people do not learn as well—or they do not learn the right things, or they do not learn much at all—when they must think and act out of compulsion rather than joy. If we understand this, then we understand a huge part of the problem. The social and cognitive sciences have made it more clear than ever that education must be relevant to the learner. The only real answer, if we want improvement, is a student-centered educational system. In a word, this means relevance.

We must go further, though, as relevance is not enough. The discussion of a "student-centered" education is where we start, not where we end. And if we don't even start there, we will go down the entirely wrong road—as I believe we have, and as I believe the substitute teacher effect shows.

—-

The substitute teacher effect is the general reaction of a student, or group of students, to a "guest teacher"—or as they often perceive it, a foreign authority figure. Though it is a small problem in and of itself, a deeper inquiry reveals that it is more a *visible sign* of a larger set of problems—including lack of understanding from adults, irrelevant curriculum, outdated methods of teaching, assessment and sorting methods that discourage rather than support, an environment saturated in extrinsic motivators, and many more cultural factors.

The substitute teacher effect is what happens when our schools and society train students to primarily follow instructions and obey authority, rather than think for themselves. It is also what happens when we build our educational strategies around a base of developmentally-inappropriate philosophies and methods. The substitute teacher effect happens because, while "play" and "socialization" are truly important in the development and life of *any* person—the students do not have nearly enough time to play and socialize during the day; we even assume that play and socialization are bad, and not as important as academic study. What happens under this mentality is that students quickly become overstressed and overworked, and must use any available time to "rest" and do things that are more personal to them, or simply to catch up on all the other sets of instructions that have been left by other teachers.

The substitute teacher effect exists because, among the various cultural reasons, students have a certain image of "school"— which we adults gave to them, in some way or another—as a painful and impersonal game to play. Quite often, they do not truly believe that the learning or "work" is in their benefit. Instead, "school" is—conciously or subconciously—perceived as something to *avoid* whenever possible, rather than an opportunity to learn what is interesting and useful to them.

When humans become locked into this kind of situation (little choice, little relevance, little joy), they will do the bare minimum to get by. (This is observable in all arenas of life.) When the substitute teacher is present, the bare minimum for students is to do "nothing at all"—or to use that time for other things—things which are more highly valued by the students than whatever they are "supposed" to be doing.

The substitute teacher effect exists because our cultural and educational methods lead to poor psychological, intellectual, and ethical health. As the students go through school, and as they grow older in our society, the effects of our extrinsic methods, insensitive demands, and often irrelevant curriculum continue to snowball. The substitute teacher arrives to find the damage that has been swept under the rug. The goal of many substitute teachers (and regular teachers) would be to sweep the problems back under the rug, as quickly and efficiently as possible. Shut them up, make them "do their work." This is essentially "classroom management," whose goal is to, as quickly as possible, declare *Problem Solved.* As we saw in this book, and can see every day in the classroom and the world, it is not actually solved. Classroom management typically hides and represses the problems. The problems grow under the surface, like mold between water-damaged walls.

—-

Some teachers, though, accept that they cannot clean up the mess, and cannot "fix" the problems. Especially the famed "sub," who will sit in their chair all day and make sure nothing truly disastrous happens—because they see nothing that can be done.

On some days, when I am too tired to be an alchemist, this is me. It will appear that I am being lazy or apathetic, when really I am simply too tired or discouraged. But on other days—when I feel strong enough, and courageous enough—I will accept the challenge, and try my best to inspire them (at least).

It is not easy, and I can never fully meet my goal. Like all other teachers, I have limited power to make a difference on my own. Though I can sometimes reach certain students, the best teacher in the world would not be enough. There are too many students, and too many problems that are created by the very structure of school and our culture. The system itself must change.

Our goal should not be to simply prevent apathy, disrespect, confusion, or chaos in the presence of the substitute teacher—or any teacher, parent, or authority figure. This would be an appeal to "band-aids;" an approach which quickly turns us into just another brick in the wall.

Our goal, as beneficent educators, is to change the very idea of school—and the ways of our world—so that people can discover what is valuable, and pursue what they value. Instead of ignoring, denying, patching, and postponing our deep systemic issues, we must offer and build upon a better system of education, and a better way of life... one that is more aligned with the true needs and desires of humanity itself.

For as long as we're relying on carrots and sticks; as long as we're ignoring student interests; as long as students are compelled to sit still and be quiet all day; as long as the "instructions" come exclusively from the "instructors;" as long as adult evaluations are the only evaluations that matter; as long as we send the message that learning must be painful; as long as play and socialization are frowned upon; as long as the reason for school is *to get a job someday*—the substitute teacher effect will persist, and it will continue to be a symptom of the greater problems.

(Book II)

This book's sequel will be an examination of motivation and assessment, and how our practices can motivate, inspire, empower, and support the health and learning of our students; or on the other hand, de-motivate, discourage, disempower, and contribute to the physical, mental, and psychological degradation of a generation—and thus, our society.

Notes & References

1 I based sections of this book, and my theory, around some ideas from the following video which contrasts Richard Ryan's and Edward Deci's "needs for self-determination" with the structure of schools (high schools in particular):
https://www.youtube.com/watch?v=T3T8pFxleyY

2 Choose one, or all three, to get an idea of some of the myths and damages of the practice of grading:
"The Case Against Grades"
http://www.alfiekohn.org/article/case-grades/
"From Degrading to De-grading"
http://www.alfiekohn.org/article/degrading-de-grading/
"Grading: The Issue is not How but Why"
http://www.alfiekohn.org/article/grading/

3 For just one example, see "Myth 19" about tracking and sorting in the book *50 Myths & Lies that Threaten America's Public Schools*, by Berliner, Glass, and Associates. The authors write: "...for the vast majority of those that are labeled in our schools as gifted and talented, or high-achieving, ability grouping by such attributes appears not to work as well as commonly thought."

4 To observe and understand an entire modern school system which is something closer to this philosophy, read *Finnish Lessons 2.0* by Pasi Sahlberg, which describes the Finnish school system, including its origins, practices, and developments.
(continued on next page)

Notes & References

4   (continued from previous page)
For examples within the United States, you can
look to many progressive schools, past or present.
Some examples would be: Montessori, Waldorf,
Dewey's "lab school" in Chicago, and other
independent schools as exemplified in the book
Loving Learning by Tom Little.

5   "For the first time in at least 50 years, a majority of
U.S. public school students come from low-income
families, according to a new analysis of 2013 federal
data, a statistic that has profound implications for
the nation."
https://www.washingtonpost.com/local/education/ma
jority-of-us-public-school-students-are-in-
poverty/2015/01/15/df7171d0-9ce9-11e4-a7ee-
526210d665b4_story.html

6   The link between poverty, health/well-being, and
academic ability seems to be one of the most
studied phenomena in the social sciences, and the
field of education research. One good summary can
be found in the segment, "How Poverty Affects
Behavior and Academic Performance":
http://www.ascd.org/publications/books/109074/cha
pters/How-Poverty-Affects-Behavior-and-Academic-
Performance.aspx

7   "America is an oligarchy, not a democracy or
republic, university study finds":
http://www.washingtontimes.com/news/2014/apr/21/
americas-oligarchy-not-democracy-or-republic-
unive/

Notes & References

8 For a six minute summary, with sources, see the
video "Corruption is Legal in America" by the
organization "Represent.Us":
https://www.youtube.com/watch?v=5tu32CCA_lg

9 A review of theory and research for the student-
centered classroom, and progressive education in
general, can be found in the article:
*"Progressive Education: Why it's hard to beat, but
also hard to find"* by Alfie Kohn:
http://www.alfiekohn.org/article/progressive-
education/
Kohn writes: "Across domains, the results
overwhelmingly favor progressive education.
Regardless of one's values, in other words, this
approach can be recommended purely on the basis
of its effectiveness."

10 This is a broader debate about the purpose of
education, teachers, and parents; it must include a
philosophical inquiry into the nature of life, living,
freedom, society, and being human. In my view, the
purpose of the teacher, adult, and society should
not be to teach by force (except in rare
circumstances). The teacher is not to "mold the
minds" of the students; the state is not to dictate,
with a few exceptions, what everyone should be
learning and doing. Adults should not dictate who
children become. Rather, adults and teachers and
society should help individuals develop themselves
in accordance to values that they come to
understand as true and beneficial. In other words,
no, it is not up to you, the teacher or parent, to
decide what, how, when, and why people are...
(continued on next page)

Notes & References

10 (continued from previous page)
...learning. It is up to you, teacher, parent, and society, to help people understand—on their own accord—what, how, when, and why to learn.
You may disagree, but then the burden will be on you to justify why you think someone else's life and development is precisely up to you, and not themselves. If you conclude that younger people, and certain people, cannot help themselves in certain circumstances—you still have the option of helping them envision and understand, rather than trying to make them a clone of your own desires.

Bonus Material:
The Story of Ricardo H.

"The Outsider"

Lots of people think I'm crazy, he told me. I was becoming something of a mentor for Ricardo, both of us being guitarists—and was surprised when he told me this. Ricardo seemed like a perfectly sane and reasonable young man. But we had gotten into a conversation about the problems with the school system. I didn't start it, by the way, he did. (I usually don't talk about this stuff with students unless they bring it up first). He told me that he was working on an art project to illustrate "Another Brick in the Wall" by Pink Floyd. He regularly talks with his friends, teachers, and family about the problems in school. Out of reaction, they tell him he is wrong.

Ricardo reminded me a lot of myself. He told me, "They say I should just accept the way it is. That I should be a "good" student, or I won't get anywhere in life. But I just want to do what is interesting to me, and make it better.... "

Some would say Ricardo is "naive," just as many people have said to me when I did not fit their expectations. Lots of people think that the boundaries cannot be broken, and you are crazy to try. But I think Ricardo is more right than most people are willing to admit.

Ricardo is in the "International Baccalaureate Programme," and we have spoken about this before—both during class and outside of class. During class I would have conversations with him and his fellow IB students while they showed me their projects. Today he would tell me that "even IB is all the same... it's just cut and paste." Now, I don't believe this is completely true, nor do I think he fully believes it—the regular classes I've seen would not allow him to do the kind of project he was doing in IB Art, and I think he knows this. But he had a major point. I have seen what they do in IB classes, and listened to the students talk about IB. It is an improvement, but not enough of a change. The stated goals of IB—its description of itself—is better than what happens in reality. That's because IB is still a part of the wider "paradigm." Ricardo is right that it is just more of the same, at least in some ways.

"I thought I was alone," Ricardo said.

"Trapped by the Wall!"

Sharpie & charcoal. 56x76 centimeters, January 2016.

by Ricardo Hernandez

"The concept of 'Breaking the Wall' is inspired by Pink Floyd's The Wall. The theme revolves around how we as individuals lose ourselves when we accept social, educational and personal pressures to change our persona. In the artwork, there is an individual who broke through the wall, but through his revolution, 'Order and Discipline' (displayed by the educated crow) came to whip him into shape (portrayed by the hammer)."

"*Hung*"
Charcoal, 61x59 centimeters, December 2015
by Ricardo Hernandez

"*Big corporations have quotas and demands to meet, and often times we as a society place the fault on them. Yet, there are always much higher factors at work that strain them. This stress is seen through the hung business man. The tree is a representation of that higher power, rooted to present international and internal affairs. It shows that there are much deeper roots to a problem than we can actually visualize or imagine.*"

"Blackout Daily"

Sharpie and colored pencils. 68x56 centimeters. May 2015

by Ricardo Hernandez

"Social indulgences often blind us from concentrating on what is important. We as a society uphold celebrities to this God-like status, portrayed by the attractive model. The media tends to revolve their stories around celebrities; who married who, who cheated on who, who did what, people know the formula. Since these people do have a cultural impact, they have a following and their opinions hold more weight."

The truth is that Ricardo is not as much an outsider as he believed. Nor am I—as people had me convinced for a long time. We all have a subconscious yearning for improvement, and a subconscious nagging that many things are wrong. It's just that a few of us are more concerned, and less willing to budge. For some of us, the problems are more visible... and more difficult to deny.

ABOUT THE AUTHOR

Sammy Kayes is a teacher, writer, musician, and activist in Chicago, Illinois. He is twenty-nine years old, and an organizer and member of various education and activist groups.

This is Sammy's first book, which was self-published. If you are a news outlet or publisher and would like to promote this book, and/or publish future works, you can find him at his website:

sammykayes.net

Sammy will also consider giving presentations at libraries, book stores, and so on.

www.ingramcontent.com/pod-product-compliance
Lightning Source LLC
Chambersburg PA
CBHW071816020426
42331CB00007B/1494